# METROPOLITAN DREAMS

## Also by Larry Millett

### Published by the University of Minnesota Press

*Minnesota Modern: Architecture and Life at Midcentury*

*Once There Were Castles: Lost Mansions and Estates of the Twin Cities*

# METROPOLITAN DREAMS

## The Scandalous Rise and Stunning Fall of a Minneapolis Masterpiece

## LARRY MILLETT

UNIVERSITY OF MINNESOTA PRESS
MINNEAPOLIS ■ LONDON

Published by the University of Minnesota Press
111 Third Avenue South, Suite 290
Minneapolis, MN 55401-2520
http://www.upress.umn.edu

Printed in the United States of America on acid-free paper

The University of Minnesota is an equal-opportunity educator and employer.

24  23  22  21  20  19  18          10  9  8  7  6  5  4  3  2  1

Library of Congress Cataloging-in-Publication Data
Millett, Larry, author.
Metropolitan dreams : the scandalous rise and stunning fall of a Minneapolis masterpiece / Larry Millett.
Minneapolis : University of Minnesota Press, 2018. | Includes bibliographical references and index.
LCCN 2018016691 | ISBN 978-1-5179-0416-6 (hc/j)
LCSH: Metropolitan Building (Minneapolis, Minn.)—History. | Mix, E. Townsend, 1831–1890. | Skyscrapers—Minnesota—Minneapolis. | Lost architecture—Minnesota—Minneapolis. | Minneapolis (Minn.)—Buildings, structures, etc.—History. | Minneapolis (Minn.)—History.
LCC NA6233.M5 N76 2018 | DDC 720/.48309776579—dc23
LC record available at https://lccn.loc.gov/2018016691

To the historic preservation community, our keepers of memory

# Contents

# INTRODUCTION

## "They Will Damn Us, They Will"

D ecember 20, 1961, was a bitter day in downtown Minneapolis, the temperature struggling to reach twelve degrees and snow swirling down from a leaden sky. But there was a job to be done, and on the rooftop of the legendary Metropolitan Building workmen bundled in heavy winter gear were preparing for a controversial act of destruction. After years of debate and a hard-fought campaign to save it, the Metropolitan was about to come down.

It was a building everyone in Minneapolis knew and many loved. A fixture at the corner of Second Avenue South and Third Street since 1890, the twelve-story Metropolitan had once been the tallest, largest, and most luxurious office building in the city. Its massive stone walls, four feet thick in places, conveyed a sense of heft and power, while its rooftop towers and parapets called to mind the jagged profile of an ancient castle. But the building was a trickster, for within its rockbound walls lay a wide-open wonder: the greatest Victorian-era light court left in the United States. Positioned beneath an enormous skylight, the court featured glass-floored galleries, ornate iron railings, and open-cage elevators that hopped from floor to floor like graceful dancers.

---

The Metropolitan Building, Third Street and Second Avenue South in downtown Minneapolis, about 1905, with the U.S. Post Office to the right. Farther down Third are the seven-story Bank of Minneapolis at Nicollet Avenue and the towered Boston Block at Hennepin Avenue. To the left along Second is the New York Life Insurance Building. Every building visible in this photograph is gone.

The building's architect, E. Townsend Mix, had enjoyed a highly successful practice in Milwaukee before moving to Minneapolis. The Metropolitan would be his last building—and his finest. Working with a lavish budget of nearly $2 million, Mix invested the building with all the grandeur he could muster, and when it formally opened in May 1890 all of Minneapolis, or so it seemed, came out to gawk at his mighty creation.

The Metropolitan had originally been known as the Northwestern Guaranty Loan Building, named after the short-lived company that built it. In the 1880s and early 1890s the company and its shadowy president, Louis Menage, soared across the financial landscape, creating a sandcastle fortune out of vast piles of debt and speculation. After less than a decade in business, the company came crashing down amid spectacular allegations of fraud and mismanagement as Menage pulled off a remarkable disappearing act that became the talk of the city.

The building, renamed in 1905 for the life insurance company that bought it, readily survived these misfortunes and went on for years as a well-occupied, if no longer first-class, office structure. Then, in the early 1950s, agitation began in earnest to clean out Minneapolis's skid row area, commonly known as the Gateway. The Metropolitan stood at the edge of this old quarter of the city that was jammed with bars, liquor stores, pawnshops, and flophouses. In 1958, following years of largely unsuccessful efforts to clean up the Gateway, the city finally approved an $18 million urban renewal plan. Largely financed by federal dollars, the ambitious plan (the largest of its kind ever undertaken in an American downtown) called for sweeping away most of the historic Gateway and redeveloping it with modern buildings.

The Minneapolis Housing and Redevelopment Authority was in charge of the project, formally known as Gateway Center Urban Renewal Plan. Despite numerous and often heated objections, the agency decided to include the Metropolitan among the approximately two hundred buildings targeted for destruction. The HRA's decision was jarring but not surprising. Old buildings, no matter their quality, were held in low esteem in the 1950s and 1960s, an era that embraced modernism in all forms.

---

The light court in the Metropolitan Building in 1959, looking toward the elevator lobbies and main staircase from the fifth floor. The man standing at the railing is unidentified.

South side of Washington Avenue, between Marquette Avenue and Second Avenue South, 1948. Hundreds of small businesses occupied the jumble of buildings that would later be swept away by the Gateway Center urban renewal project.

But the Metropolitan wasn't just any old building. With its dazzling light court, it was a nationally significant work of architecture, and the plan to wreck it touched off the first big historic preservation fight in the city's history. It was waged before the HRA's board, at Minneapolis City Council meetings, in letters to the editor in local newspapers, and in the offices of state and local politicians. At a time when few historic preservation laws existed and the courts were not inclined to challenge urban renewal programs, those opposing demolition of the Metropolitan had little hope of success. The HRA seemed almost desperately intent on destroying the building and refused to make any concessions as one court and then another ruled in its favor.

By October 1961, as the HRA evicted the building's last tenants, the battle

Demolition worker Dennis Carlyle wields a sledgehammer atop the Metropolitan Building as demolition begins on December 20, 1961. The clock tower of Minneapolis City Hall looms in the background.

was lost, and for the next two months the Metropolitan, vacant and forlorn, became the most famous architectural corpse in the Twin Cities, a shuttered symbol of the old Gateway and its impending doom. Photographers scurried to record the building's every detail; newspaper columnists mourned its fate; and architectural historians from across the country wrote last-minute letters of protest, to no avail.

When the wreckers finally arrived, photographers from the *Minneapolis Tribune* and its afternoon sibling, the *Star,* were on hand to record the moment that had been long dreaded in some quarters and long awaited in others. According to the *Tribune,* a workman named Dale La Roche struck the first sledgehammer blow to the building's sandstone parapets. The *Star* attributed the initial attack to

Ruins of the Metropolitan Building in 1962, toward the entrance on Second Avenue South. The rock-faced walls of New Hampshire granite that formed the lower three floors were four feet thick.

---

another worker, Dennis Carlyle. "For the next four months," the *Tribune* reported, "men with crowbars and sledgehammers, wrecking ball and demolition hooks, will crash and batter at the relic until it is a pile of rubble." In fact, it took eight months to bring the building down.[1]

The day before demolition began, the *Tribune* interviewed Wally Marotzke, who had been a janitor in the building since the early 1940s. Marotzke acknowledged that the Metropolitan was a faded beauty, tarnished by time and circumstance. Yet like so many others who worked in the building, he had found in it some elemental magic, and he knew its like would never be seen again. "I'm not gonna watch 'em rip it down," he told the *Tribune*'s reporter. "I don't think I could. But I'll tell you one thing: the future generations are gonna read about this building, and they'll see some of the buildings they're putting up here and they will damn us, they will, for tearing down the Met."[2]

The janitor spoke the truth.

# "Risen like an Exhalation"

In January 1889, as the dark stone walls of the Northwestern Guaranty Loan Building rose toward the sky, a newspaper reporter wrote that "to comprehend the magnitude of the growth of Minneapolis is almost beyond the power of the average person." Newspapers of the era were prone to all manner of hype and exaggeration, but in this instance the reporter could not be faulted for overstating the case. Minneapolis in the 1880s had indeed experienced a remarkable urban efflorescence, and the Guaranty Loan Building was in many ways the culminating symbol of a decade that utterly transformed the city.[1]

In 1870 Minneapolis was a small prairie town of 13,000 people. Just twenty years later, it was the nation's eighteenth-largest city, with a population of 165,000. The greatest surge of all occurred during the 1880s, when the city added 118,000 people and 30,000 or more new buildings. This astonishing torrent of growth came so quickly and with such force that it must have seemed little short of miraculous to those who lived through it.

"Minneapolis has risen like an exhalation," the architecture critic Montgomery Schuyler wrote after a visit in 1890. Stunned by what he had seen, Schuyler wrote that Minneapolis was "a city where antiquity means the day before yesterday, and posterity the day after to-morrow, the present is the most contemptible of tenses, and men inevitably come to think and live and build in the future-perfect." Schuyler noted that St. Paul, which Minneapolis eclipsed in population by 1880, had evolved through the usual stages of urban growth after its founding in the

9

Minneapolis, south across Nicollet Island, circa 1870. The first Hennepin Avenue Suspension Bridge, built in 1855, is at far right. Louis Menage arrived in the city about this time and soon began buying and selling real estate.

1830s. Minneapolis, by contrast, seemed to have "sprung from the heads of its projectors full-panoplied in brick and mortar."[2]

Schuyler's comments, while perhaps a bit too fully panoplied in their own right, captured the exuberant spirit of Minneapolis in the 1880s, when Louis Menage founded the Northwestern Guaranty Loan Company and a few years later began building its monumental new home. By the time he occupied his luxurious suite of offices on the tenth floor in 1890, Menage was at the summit of his career, with prospects as expansive as the view from his windows. A compulsive optimist, Menage saw a future without limits for himself and for the city where he had made his fortune.

Menage was not alone in his optimism. The future appeared so blindingly bright that the *Minneapolis Tribune* predicted the city might well have a million or more people by 1902. In fact, the city barely climbed past the two hundred thousand mark at the turn of the century, and a bitter depression that began in 1893 doused many dreams. Menage's fall, as it turned out, would be especially hard, leaving in its wake a trail of financial wreckage that extended all across the United States.[3]

Throughout the 1880s, however, both Menage and Minneapolis were on the rise. As the decade began, Minneapolis was a city of forty-seven thousand people. Although it had already experienced spasms of rapid growth, it did not have the look or feel of a big city. Its municipal boundaries encompassed only 12.5 square miles, including the old town of St. Anthony (absorbed into Minneapolis in 1874) on the east side of the Mississippi River. The land beyond Twenty-Sixth Avenue North and what would become Lake Street to the south remained outside the city limits and was still rural in character.

The lakes that one day would become the pride of the city remained largely undeveloped, although Menage, who had real estate interests in the lake district, would within a few years assume ownership of the Lyndale Hotel, an early resort on the eastern shore of Lake Calhoun (now Bde Maka Ska, the original Dakota name for the lake). Lake of the Isles was still a swamp, and Lake Nokomis was a duck pond no more than four feet deep. There were few houses and as yet no parks around any of these bodies of water.

Most residents of the city lived close to the downtown core, within walking distance of where they worked. Horsecar lines, slow and not always reliable, provided the only form of mass transit. By 1880 a rudimentary network of routes extended as far as Plymouth Avenue on the north and Franklin Avenue on the south. There was also a narrow-gauge commuter rail line, built in 1879, that connected downtown to Lake Calhoun. Formally known as the Minneapolis, Lyndale and Minnetonka Railway, it lasted for only a few years amid mounting complaints about soot, smoke, and noise.

The city's compact downtown, served by dirt streets and wooden sidewalks, was centered in the Gateway area. No firm boundaries defined the Gateway, but in time it came to be viewed as the area from roughly Second Avenue North to Fourth Avenue South, and from the Mississippi River to about Third Street. Its early focal point was Bridge Square at the intersection of Washington and Hennepin Avenues. The square took its name from the nearby Hennepin Avenue Suspension Bridge. Built in 1855, the bridge was until 1874 the city's only vehicular crossing of the Mississippi River, linking Minneapolis to St. Anthony on the east

Bridge Square and Minneapolis City Hall, circa 1875. The square was a large, sharply angled intersection where Hennepin Avenue (at right) and Nicollet Avenue came together. Gateway Park took up much of the area after the city hall was demolished in 1912.

bank. It was all but inevitable that a downtown would develop close to this vital river crossing.

The establishment of a downtown district in Minneapolis followed the typical American pattern, which was much different from that of most European cities, where stores, offices, and other commercial buildings were widely scattered and shop owners often lived above their businesses. Americans generally preferred to live in homes separate from their places of business or employment. As a result, commercial life tended to concentrate in well-defined cores occupied by stores, offices, and major public buildings. Horsecar (and later streetcar) lines converged in these cores, making them the busy center of city life. The word "downtown" did not appear in dictionaries until the early 1900s, by which time every American city of any size already had just such a place.[4]

Downtown Minneapolis in 1880 could hardly be described as impressive. Small brick and stone commercial buildings, most from two to four stories high and occupying lots that were often no more than twenty-five feet wide, clustered around Bridge Square and along nearby Washington Avenue. These buildings offered little in the way of architectural pretense and followed the standard architectural styles of the time, if any at all.

In 1873 the square acquired its most monumental building, a mansard-roofed city hall that almost immediately proved too small to meet the needs of the rapidly growing city and its government. Hennepin County, meanwhile, made do with a small, 1850s-vintage courthouse at Fourth Street and Chicago Avenue, well away from the heart of downtown. By the end of the 1880s, work began on a combined city hall and county courthouse, known as the Municipal Building, which

Nicollet Avenue and Second Street (in foreground), circa 1880. By this time the Gateway area was the densest part of Minneapolis, with hundreds of small brick and stone commercial buildings lining the streets.

Nicollet House Hotel, Washington Avenue between Nicollet and Hennepin Avenues, circa 1880. The oldest section of the hotel, dating to 1858, is at right. With its distinctive twin cupolas, the Nicollet was a downtown landmark for many years.

would dwarf its crude predecessors and provide yet another visible demonstration of how far Minneapolis had advanced in just a decade.

Although Bridge Square served as the initial focal point of downtown Minneapolis, Washington Avenue between about Second Avenue North and Third Avenue South soon developed into a prime commercial area as well. At one hundred feet wide, Washington was the city's broadest street (most other downtown streets were eighty feet) and its prominence was such that it became the route of the city's first horsecar line in 1875. Washington would later become notorious for its flophouses and bars, but in the early 1880s it was a prime commercial street lined with rows of tightly packed brick buildings, including many of the city's largest banks. Much of the Gateway had a similar character, offering a mix of stores, warehouses, office buildings, and transient hotels.[5]

Building permits weren't required in Minneapolis until 1884, and the history of many of the early buildings in the Gateway is obscure. But maps show most blocks within the district were already filled with buildings by the time the first permits were issued. The largest downtown building at the beginning of the 1880s was in all likelihood the Nicollet House Hotel, which stretched for an entire block along Washington between Hennepin and Nicollet Avenues. Five stories high, it came equipped with one of the city's first passenger elevators.

A remarkable aspect of the Gateway, which was home to hundreds of buildings constructed before 1890, is how long much of it survived. This happened not because of any organized preservation efforts but because new downtown development after 1900 largely shifted to the south as the Gateway descended into a skid row. So much of the district's historic core remained in the 1950s that entire blocks filled with buildings had to be cleared to make way for the Gateway Center urban renewal project and other new developments.

As the Gateway solidified into a commercial district, much of the rest of what is now downtown Minneapolis was occupied by housing of all kinds, including numerous mansions. Real estate mogul Samuel Gale built one of the city's first Italianate-style mansions in 1864 at Fourth Street and Marquette Avenue. By the 1870s scores of other big houses appeared along Fifth, Sixth, Seventh, and Eighth Streets South. One of the largest, William Judd's 1873 towered brick mansion on Fifth Street near Portland Avenue, was set amid grounds occupying an entire block. These early mansions, although big on architectural pretense, were modest by later standards, and a home with five thousand square feet would have been considered palatial in the day.

Most housing in the downtown area was far more modest, ranging from tiny cottages to simple wood-frame houses to crowded tenements. In many cases, homes were intermixed with commercial buildings, since comprehensive zoning did not arrive in Minneapolis until the 1920s. Even as commercial development spread, many parts of downtown remained heavily residential well into the 1880s. The block bounded by Second and Third Avenues South and Fifth and Sixth Streets, for example, was still filled with houses—eighteen in all—as late as 1885.

But by the time Samuel Gale moved to a new mansion near Loring Park in

Mansions along Seventh Street at Third Avenue South, circa 1875. Outsized houses once filled many blocks in downtown Minneapolis, but the grandeur was accompanied by wooden sidewalks and dirt streets. The towered Italianate mansion at the corner was built around 1870 by John W. Day.

1888, downtown's old urban order was already being crushed under the pressure of a building boom so powerful that the local newspapers, which usually dished out superlatives like heaping plates of cheap spaghetti, seemed finally at a loss for words. Wrote a reporter for the *Tribune*, "She [Minneapolis] has broken over all former records of her own making. In many branches it is impossible to estimate how great her growth has been. In some, where estimates are possible, the results of these estimates seem so nearly impossible that many will hesitate to confess to believe in them."[6]

The grand opening of the Northwestern Guaranty Loan Building on May 31, 1890, was as much a celebration of the astounding growth of the city as of the building itself. Some among the thousands of visitors who poured into the building had arrived via the new electric streetcars that were quickly revolutionizing mass transit. The city's first electrified line had begun operation on December 24, 1889, running down Third Street directly past the building. New lines spread rapidly through downtown and the rest of the city, and wherever they looked riders would have seen an extraordinary spectacle of progress.

The big construction boom in Minneapolis actually began in about 1878 or 1879, after the effects of a severe recession caused by the Panic of 1873 had finally worn off. In 1881 alone, more than three thousand new buildings were erected in the city, the vast majority of them houses. The peak of the boom occurred between 1884 and 1888, when at least twenty-one thousand buildings were constructed in Minneapolis. The city's boundaries also grew quickly, with forty square miles of territory added through annexation in the 1880s.[7]

Immigration fueled the huge growth in population that in turn fed the building boom. Scandinavians led the way. In 1880 only about two hundred Johnsons appeared in the annual *Davison City Directory* for Minneapolis. A decade later, the directory listed more than two thousand people with that surname living in the city.

Many of these immigrants found employment in the milling district around St. Anthony Falls. The dense collection of stone and brick mills there for a time formed the most impressive architectural ensemble in Minneapolis. Twenty-five flour mills, the bulk of them lined up along a power canal on the west side of the falls, produced two million barrels annually by 1880, while twenty or so sawmills

Streetcars on Third Street, circa 1890, moving past the recently completed Northwestern Guaranty Loan Building. Electric streetcars were introduced in Minneapolis in December 1889, and the tracks here temporarily had three rails after being converted from narrow to standard gauge to accommodate the new trolleys.

---

cut 180 million board feet of lumber from the northern pineries. These numbers would grow markedly over the next decade, with flour production tripling and lumber output doubling. Two gigantic new mills (the Washburn A, built in 1880, and the Pillsbury A, completed a year later) provided much of this additional flour power and served as early evidence that Minneapolis was a city primed for growth.[8]

The railroads were another huge employer. A half-dozen lines had trackage in the city by 1880 and more would soon follow. The completion in 1883 of the St. Paul, Minneapolis and Manitoba (later Great Northern) Railway's monumental Stone Arch Bridge across St. Anthony Falls demonstrated the newfound might of the railroads. Two years later, the city's first consolidated Union Depot opened at the foot of Hennepin Avenue.

Although the entire city became a supercharged engine of growth in the 1880s, the downtown area saw some of the greatest changes. A southward march occurred as new buildings rose along Hennepin, Nicollet, and Marquette Avenues away from the historic core at Bridge Square. Older buildings, among them numerous houses, were quickly swept away by this surging commercial tide. Some houses were demolished but many others were moved. By 1885 at least twenty-three firms in Minneapolis specialized in house moving, and the sight of homes wheeling through the streets became so common that it attracted little notice.

As the downtown area expanded, commercial buildings grew ever taller and larger. The *Tribune* noted in 1881, "The day of the three-story blocks it is hoped has gone by for Minneapolis." The newspaper was at least partly right. Although many small commercial blocks of three or fewer stories were erected in the 1880s, higher buildings in the six- to twelve-story range began to appear by the early years of the decade. Today, these would be called midrise buildings, but at the time their unprecedented height made them seem like a new breed of architectural giants. The Guaranty Loan Building was in every sense the culmination of what might be called the early skyscraper age in Minneapolis.[9]

Tall office buildings and hotels of six stories or more had first appeared in New York around 1870, but it wasn't until the booming 1880s that such buildings

Flour mills in Minneapolis, circa 1885. By this time the city's West Side milling district at St. Anthony Falls was the largest in the world, with twenty-five flour mills in operation. A trestle built for the Minneapolis Western Railroad extends in front of the mills.

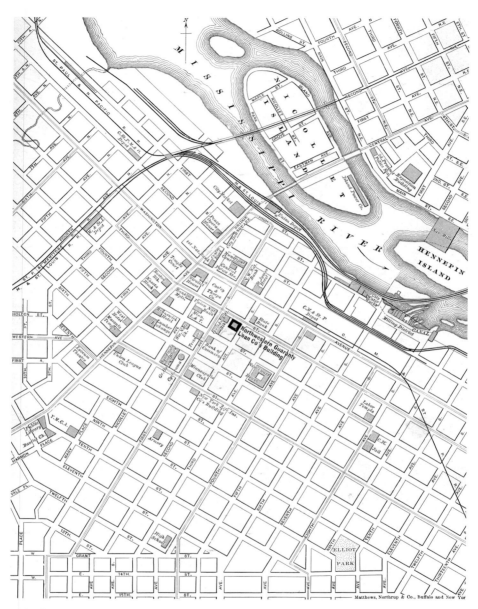

Major buildings in downtown Minneapolis, 1890. This map originally appeared in a book commemorating the Northwestern Guaranty Loan Building.

Boston Block, Third Street and Hennepin Avenue, circa 1886. When it opened in 1881, the Boston Block was among the first office buildings in Minneapolis to reach five stories and to be equipped with passenger elevators.

became a common sight in cities around the country. In Minneapolis, the age of tall downtown buildings began with the Boston Block, designed by prominent Minneapolis architect Leroy Buffington and built in 1881 at Third Street and Hennepin Avenue. It was only five stories high (it would be expanded to seven stories after a fire in 1887), but its size and massiveness were unprecedented in Minneapolis. The building included at least one passenger elevator, possibly the first installed in a Minneapolis office building.

Other, taller buildings soon followed. All told, twenty-one buildings of six stories or more were constructed in downtown Minneapolis by 1890. The Lumber Exchange at Fifth Street and Hennepin Avenue, completed in 1886, was the first of this early batch of tall office structures to reach ten stories and was the city's highest building until the Guaranty Loan became king of the downtown skyline. The Lumber Exchange still stands (with two stories added in 1909), but most of the other early high-rise buildings in downtown Minneapolis are long gone.

Hennepin Avenue, now a street best known for theaters and bars, was the epicenter of the city's initial boom in tall office buildings. Between 1884 and

1889, nine buildings between six and ten stories high were built along Hennepin. The Lumber Exchange and the Masonic Temple are the only survivors from this group, which included the West Hotel, the Kasota Block, and Temple Court. The eight-story Temple Court, at Hennepin and Washington Avenues, was especially intriguing. Completed in 1886, it was architect E. Townsend Mix's first office building in Minneapolis and, like his later Guaranty Loan Building, featured a striking interior light court.

It is hard now to comprehend just how revolutionary these tall buildings were in their day. Designed around elevators and featuring iron or steel frames, they allowed developers to make greater use than they ever had before of increasingly expensive downtown land. In the 1860s, the entire block on which the Guaranty Loan Building was constructed would have cost about $1,800. By 1888, when a quarter of the block was purchased as the site for the building, the price was $210,000.[10]

∼

Skyscrapers weren't the only new building type introduced to Minneapolis in the 1880s. The luxury hotel also made its entrance with the completion of the West at Fifth and Hennepin in 1884. The city's earlier hotels, such as the Nicollet House, which opened its doors in 1858, had been relatively crude structures, with small rooms, limited bathroom facilities, and modest lobbies. The West, another creation by architect Leroy Buffington, was far more luxurious and sophisticated than any of its predecessors in Minneapolis.

Built by a hotel magnate from Cincinnati named Charles West and his nephew, John West, the hotel was eight stories high, making it the city's tallest building before the Lumber Exchange. Its architecture was richly picturesque, with a profusion of gables, dormers, and chimneys animating the roofline. Within there was a two-story, skylit lobby, which the owners advertised, perhaps with more hope than accuracy, as the largest in the country. The West offered 407 rooms (about a quarter of which came with private baths), a vast Moorish-style banquet hall, a well-appointed barroom, and many other amenities.

Louis Menage was a resident of the West for several years in the mid-1880s, and for a time he maintained offices a short walk away in the six-story Kasota Block, built in 1884 at Fourth and Hennepin. E. Townsend Mix also lived at the West, which functioned both as a residential and transient hotel. Never a great

West Hotel, Fifth Street and Hennepin Avenue, circa 1900. The West, built in 1884, was Minneapolis's first grand hotel. E. Townsend Mix, architect of the Guaranty Loan Building, lived here after moving to Minneapolis in the late 1880s.

financial success, the West suffered extensive damage in a 1906 fire that claimed at least eight and possibly ten lives, and it went downhill from there. It was razed in 1940—one of the first great downtown monuments of the 1880s to fall to the wrecker.[11]

～

Hennepin, Nicollet, and Marquette Avenues were the main corridors of downtown's southward expansion. Business blocks, as they were called in the day, drove much of the new development, especially along Nicollet. The mightiest of these was the five-story Syndicate Block, which opened in 1883 and extended from Fifth to Sixth Streets along the east side of Nicollet Avenue. Said to offer five

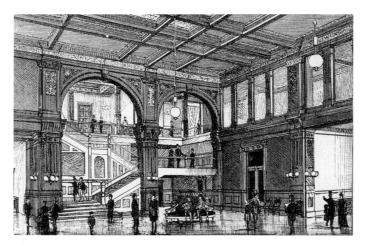

(*Above*) Lobby of the West Hotel, circa 1887. A skylight atop the two-story lobby brought in daylight through a large well at the center of the building. (*Right*) Syndicate Block, Nicollet Avenue, between Fifth and Sixth Streets, circa 1905. The massive Syndicate Block was one of several new buildings along Nicollet that led to a southward shift of downtown's commercial core in the 1880s. The towered building farther down Nicollet was the headquarters of the Minnesota Loan and Trust Company, built in 1885.

acres of floor space, the building was touted as "the largest block under one roof in America." It's highly unlikely this was true, but the Syndicate Block certainly dwarfed any other retail structure in Minneapolis. One of its primary tenants was John Bradstreet, a prominent interior designer whose furniture store occupied the central portion of the building.

The building took its name from the syndicate of a dozen leading Minneapolis businessmen who financed the project. As was quite common at the time, the syndicate staged an architectural competition to design the building. Mix, then still based in Milwaukee, was among those invited to submit plans. He didn't win—the commission went to the Minneapolis firm of Kees and Fisk—but it was likely Mix's initial attempt to secure a foothold in the Minneapolis commercial market.[12]

A nearby retailer also proved to be a significant factor in the southward shift of downtown. Donaldson's Department Store, founded by brothers William and Lawrence Donaldson, opened in 1881 in a modest one-story building at Sixth Street and Nicollet Avenue. At that time, the store was something of an outlier among the city's major retailers, most of which were still located in the Gateway. The construction two years later of the Syndicate Block just across Sixth Street proved that the Donaldsons had chosen their location wisely. In 1888 the brothers

Donaldson's Glass Block Department Store, Sixth Street and Nicollet Avenue, 1925. Built in 1888, the Glass Block was downtown Minneapolis's first big department store. The Gateway area a few blocks to the north remained vibrant at this time but gradually lost cachet as other large retailers began opening new stores near Donaldson's.

tore down their cramped old building and replaced it with the five-story "Glass Block," which instantly became the largest and most luxurious department store in the city.[13]

~

As the commercial district continued its relentless expansion through the 1880s, new residential construction moved largely to the peripheries of downtown or to other parts of the city. Some of the most lavish mansions in the history of Minneapolis were built during this period. The Loring and Elliot Park neighborhoods, Hawthorne Avenue, Tenth Street South, and to a lesser extent Lowry Hill (much of which didn't fill in until the 1890s), became the sites of scores of new homes. Even so, a few big houses were built close to the commercial core as late as 1898, when George C. Christian moved into a new mansion on Eighth Street near Fifth Avenue South.

Beard's Block, Washington Avenue at Eleventh Avenue South, circa 1876. With more than sixty apartments, Beard's Block was one of Minneapolis's earliest tenements. Many others were built in and around downtown as the city's population exploded in the 1880s.

Small houses on Fourth Avenue South near Fourth Street, circa 1890s. Downtown Minneapolis in the late nineteenth century was an architectural free-for-all. These workers' cottages stood almost within the shadow of the Guaranty Loan Building before being torn down in the early 1900s to make way for commercial development.

Some of the city's wealthiest families had already moved out of the downtown area by the mid-1880s. William Washburn, a businessman and politician who had built a house in the 1860s at 503 Seventh Street South, relocated in 1884 to a vast new mansion at Stevens Avenue and Twenty-Second Street, well south of downtown, in what would later be called the Washburn–Fair Oaks neighborhood. Mix designed the mansion, establishing a connection to Washburn that would significantly further his career in Minneapolis. Park Avenue south of Sixteenth Street became another favored locale for mansions during this period.

Although hundreds of single-family homes could still be found throughout the downtown area in the 1880s, apartments, ranging from cheaply built tenements to ultraluxurious row houses, became increasingly popular as the city's population swelled. Beard's Block, built between 1876 and 1881 at Washington and Eleventh Avenues South, with more than sixty apartments was by far the

Washburn Apartments, Eighth Street South and Portland Avenue, following a fire, 1944. Louis Menage built the apartments, which still stand, in 1888. He and his family occupied a deluxe multistory unit with more than twenty rooms before moving into a new house on Lowry Hill in the early 1890s.

largest of the tenements. All told, at least sixty row houses were built in the downtown area and its immediate environs in the 1880s. These dwellings popped up everywhere, even in the heart of the commercial district. Among them was a two-story, wood-frame tenement that until about 1900 stood across from the Guaranty Loan Building on Second Avenue South.

Relatively few row houses or apartment buildings from the 1880s remain in downtown Minneapolis today. Among the survivors is a rather nondescript brick building at 610 Eighth Street South now known as the Washburn Apartments. When it opened in 1888, it contained several spacious, multistory units, one of which was occupied by Menage, his wife, and his daughter. Menage had in fact built the apartments, which were sometimes referred to as "Menage's Tenement." It appears he lived in the building until early 1893, when he and his family moved into a new house on Lowry Hill.[14]

~

There may never have been a more interesting time to be in downtown Minneapolis than the 1880s. Intensely dynamic, it was place of extraordinary variety and great extremes. With no zoning regulations in effect, downtown was a wild jumble of buildings. Shacks stood next to skyscrapers, churches jostled against shops and stores, back alleys housed a bewildering array of sheds and stables, and even a structure as monumental as the Syndicate Block for a time overlooked nothing more grand than a roller-skating rink.

The block that became home to the Guaranty Loan Building, bounded by Third and Fourth Streets and Marquette and Second Avenues South, displayed just such a mix of uses. An 1885 atlas shows that the north half of the block, along Third, was largely vacant, in part because a sizable lot at the corner of Marquette had already been acquired for the site of a new U.S. Post Office, completed in 1889. Meanwhile, the Guaranty Loan Building's future site at Third Street and Second Avenue South housed only two small commercial buildings, both of which would be cleared away in 1888.

The south half of the block, along Fourth, was entirely different, with twenty or more brick or wood-frame structures already in place. The lineup included A. W. Hapgood's Livery Stable along the alley, the four-story Cascade Steam Laundry, several store buildings, a large double house, and five small dwellings, two of which were set well back from the street behind other structures. This mishmash would give way by 1900 to a somewhat tidier collection of commercial buildings, and that has been the essential developmental order of downtown ever since, as small buildings are replaced by ever larger ones. Today many downtown blocks are occupied by a single building; in 1885 some blocks had thirty or more.

The downtown of the 1880s, although it offered much elegant architecture, was also a place of ragged edges, dark corners, and open vice. Along First Street South, not far from the site of the Guaranty Loan Building, a flourishing red-light district was home to fifteen brothels, some of which offered their carnal delights in an atmosphere of considerable refinement. Nettie Conley, one of the city's most successful madams, spiffed up her establishment with the help of a $6,000 loan from John Bradstreet, who may have provided furnishings and design advice as part of the arrangement.[15]

Gambling dens, usually well positioned on the upper floors or in the back

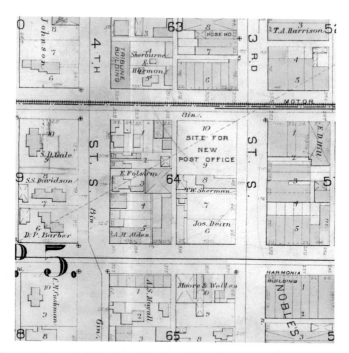

Site of the Guaranty Loan Building from Hopkins Atlas of Minneapolis, 1885. The northern half of the block, which included the site for the new U.S. Post Office, was largely vacant. William Washburn purchased the quarter-block lot at Second Avenue South and Third Street, where the Guaranty Loan Building began rising in 1888, for $210,000.

rooms of saloons, also thrived at a time when the city's police force does not appear to have been especially eagle-eyed. In 1888, for example, the *Minneapolis Tribune* reported the doleful tale of two young brothers who were fleeced out of $225, their entire savings, at "the well known gambling house over Paul Schmedeman's saloon at 205 Nicollet avenue." The brothers went on several occasions to the city's redoubtable superintendent of police, Jacob Hein, to complain. Hein eventually claimed he had done his best to discover the owners of the illegal gambling hall but that his herculean efforts failed because no one "would admit him to the room."[16]

Meanwhile, another group of public servants—the fire department—had no shortage of work. Fires were extremely common and often lethal in the downtown of the 1880s. Although Minneapolis had early on established fire limits that outlawed construction of wood-frame structures in the heart of downtown, even

Ruins of the Tribune Building, Marquette Avenue and Fourth Street, 1889. Seven newspaper employees died and many others were injured when fire swept through the seven-story building in November 1889. The building, constructed in 1885, had only one staircase and many of the victims were trapped on the upper floors.

---

supposedly fireproof masonry and iron-frame buildings were hardly immune to the threat of going up in flames. Building permits for downtown addresses show that fires large and small struck with daunting regularity. The decade drew to a close with what remains the deadliest office-building fire in the city's history. The fire, on November 30, 1889, destroyed the seven-story Tribune Building, constructed just four years earlier at Fourth Street and Marquette Avenue. Seven newspaper employees died in the fire and many others were injured.

The Guaranty Loan Building was nearing completion when the Tribune Building, just a block away, burned down. Although the Tribune had been a substantial structure, it was small and rather crude compared to the Guaranty Loan. Menage had from the start wanted his new building to be a powerful statement, and when it opened one commentator likened it to a "small red mountain" towering over the city. Its rugged walls of granite and sandstone did indeed give the building a dense, lithic presence, as though it had been hewn from a mighty rock formation. But the truth was that it had been built out of airy speculation, the product of an all but incomprehensible empire of finance devised and managed by one of the most fascinating figures in the history of Minneapolis.

Sawmills at St. Anthony Falls, circa 1870. Louis Menage spent one summer working at a sawmill in Minneapolis before embarking on his career in real estate and finance.

# "A Man of Peculiar Genius and Business Methods"

Louis Menage was just twenty-one years old when he arrived in Minneapolis in 1871 with little cash in his pocket and few prospects. Like many of the city's early settlers, he was a New Englander, born in Rhode Island and raised in Massachusetts. Although his lineage was impressive enough—his father was of French ancestry, his mother a descendant of the original Pilgrim colony in New England—Menage had not come from wealth. His father, who operated a confectionery business in New Bedford, Massachusetts, died when Menage was in his teens, and his mother succumbed not long thereafter to tuberculosis. Menage showed early signs of being afflicted by the same disease, and part of his reason for moving to Minneapolis was to reap the supposed benefits of its dry, cold climate.

Menage's career in Minnesota began inauspiciously. He taught shorthand for a time at a business college in Minneapolis, then spent two winters in the northern pineries as a clerk and timekeeper for a logging camp on Lake Pokegama near Grand Rapids. He also worked one summer for a sawmill at St. Anthony Falls and as early as 1872 began dabbling in real estate in Minneapolis. He was clearly precocious when it came to business and finance, and it's likely he was largely self-taught, since it does not appear he had extensive formal schooling. After his second stint in the North Woods, Menage returned to Minneapolis in 1873 and began buying and selling real estate as a full-time occupation. By August of that year, he was advertising regularly in the *Minneapolis Tribune,* offering lots for sale for $400 an acre on Hennepin Avenue "but a few rods from the city limits."[1]

The essential mystery of Menage's career is how quickly he was able to establish himself in the real estate business. In the winter of 1872–73 he was an obscure young clerk toiling at the frigid edge of nowhere. A few months later, at the ripe age of twenty-three, he had turned himself into an apparently well-capitalized real estate broker, with offices in the heart of the bustling Gateway district.[2]

Well after Menage's fall from grace, the *Chicago Tribune* described him as "a man of peculiar genius and business methods," and it was not meant as a compliment. Menage clearly possessed something like genius when it came to manipulating money, but he often did so in a way that, even in the freebooting days of the 1880s, went well beyond the usual bounds of sharp practice. Leverage, much of it in the form of debt instruments of highly dubious quality, was at the core of everything Menage did during his career in Minneapolis, and as time went on his financial dealings spiraled into such baroque complexity that they all but defied comprehension.[3]

Menage had one other notable skill. He was able, early on, to align himself with men of wealth and influence, and those connections helped launch him on a quick path to success in Minneapolis. Some of the city's leading businessmen, from Thomas Lowry to William Washburn to members of the Pillsbury family, were drawn into Menage's swirling orbit, to their ultimate regret.

Another reason for Menage's rapid rise was that he was in the right business in the right place at the right time. Real estate was a kind of earthen gold in the early days of Minneapolis, and much of the city's financial life revolved around it, the universal assumption being that prices, aside from a brief dip now and then, would always trend upward. By 1873, when a financial panic did indeed depress the market for a time, there were already 30 real estate dealers in the city. Just ten years later, there were 213.[4]

Although little is known about Menage's early real estate ventures, one trait that would mark his entire career—relatively frugal living—was already in evidence. Menage in 1873 resided in a run-of-the-mill boardinghouse in Southeast Minneapolis, and even as his business grew and the money poured in, he showed little interest in the opulent lifestyle of many of his peers. By all accounts, Menage worked obsessively, sometimes around the clock, and playing with money seems

Snyder and McFarlane Real Estate Office, Minneapolis, 1856. Buying and selling real estate was big business in every frontier city. By 1873 thirty real estate dealers were at work in Minneapolis and within a decade there would be more than two hundred.

to have been the game he enjoyed above all others. When Menage built the Guaranty Loan Building, he spared no expense because it was intended as a monument to his business success. The house he built three years later on Mount Curve Avenue was, by contrast, so unassuming that it made little impression amid the often fulsome mansions of Lowry Hill. Still, as time went on, Menage indulged in some luxuries, among them a summer place on Lake Calhoun.

Menage's solo career in real estate did not last long. In May 1874 he went into partnership with Henry C. Brackett, a long-established real estate dealer in Minneapolis. Brackett also owned and managed the Clark House Hotel, on Hennepin Avenue at Fourth Street, where Menage soon took up residence. The firm of Brackett and Menage initially did business at 241 Marquette Avenue but relocated to offices on the ground floor of the Nicollet House Hotel. "What Mr. Brackett doesn't know about Minneapolis real estate is not worth knowing," the *Tribune* reported in announcing the partnership, "and we have no doubt the firm will have immense success." It's not clear whether the firm did indeed fulfill that rosy prediction, but by the end of 1874 Menage was already deep into his first big project.[5]

In December of that year, Menage began platting Lake Side Park, a large tract of land on the west side of Lake Calhoun, where the Minikahda Club now stands. The site was platted with huge lots—some along the lakeshore had two hundred feet of frontage—and was designed to serve as an upscale suburban retreat filled with expansive homes. But the project never took off, nor was a resort hotel Menage later built on the property a success. The problem was getting there: only a single road reached around to the west side of the lake in the 1870s, and the site was simply too remote to attract development.[6]

Despite its poor showing, Lake Side Park served as a template for Menage's career in real estate. His strategy, carried out in numerous subdivisions that bore his name, was to acquire farmland near the edge of the city, plat it, and then sell the lots for housing. It didn't take him long to figure out that the ultralarge lots he had platted at Lake Side Park were difficult to sell, and most of his subsequent developments featured smaller lots intended for a middle-class clientele. By the 1880s Menage was among Minneapolis's leading property developers, a remarkable ascendancy given that he was still barely in his thirties.

In 1876 Menage took time out from his real estate activities to do some courting, and in September of that year he married Amanda Bull. Their only child, a

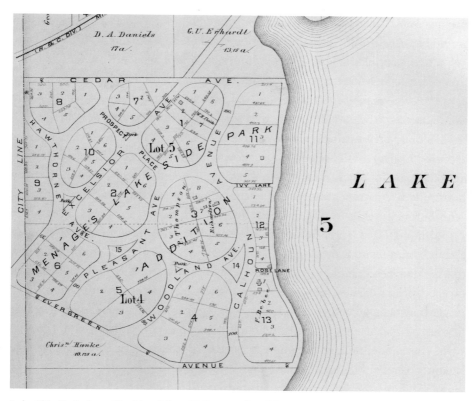

Lake Side Park, from Hopkins Atlas of Minneapolis, 1885. Louis Menage platted the residential development on the west side of Lake Calhoun in the early 1870s, but it was never a success.

daughter named Bessie, was born a year later. The marriage offered Menage yet another link to the upper echelons of the city's business class. Amanda's father, Benjamin S. Bull, had arrived in Minneapolis in the founding days of the city in 1855, and his résumé included stints as a wholesale grocer, a flour miller, and the owner of a Montana silver mine. In 1882 Bull became a partner in Menage's real estate firm and later served as an officer of the Northwestern Guaranty Loan Company.[7]

Menage ultimately platted and sold thousands of residential lots in Minneapolis, mostly in and around the lake district. All of them had one thing in common—an unusual and, as it turned out, profitable deed restriction. Menage was a Baptist and strict prohibitionist, and the deeds to his properties came with a clause barring the owner from making, selling, or keeping for sale on the premises any "spiritous, vinous, malt or brewed liquors." Violating this provision would cause title to the property to be forfeited back to Menage.

Since it's unlikely Menage ever employed teams of agents to hunt down basement distilleries, there was little means of enforcing the clause. Even so, it became an issue as properties were sold and resold. Mortgage lenders were wary of the clause, which clouded the title, and so Menage, his wife, and later his daughter did a tidy little business signing releases for a fee. A Minneapolis newspaper reported in 1929 that Bessie Menage, then living in New Jersey, charged an average of $25 per lot to wipe away the restriction. By one estimate the Menages may have collected as much $100,000 in release payments over the course of many years before the clause was finally invalidated in the 1950s.[8]

Although Menage became very successful in real estate, his business went through hard times following the Panic of 1873. The panic, which turned into a full-fledged depression, was touched off in September of that year when a bank owned by the financier Jay Cooke failed. Newspaper notices from 1876 and 1877 reveal that Menage began defaulting on mortgages as business fell off. He also lost his partner, Henry Brackett, who left the firm for unknown reasons in June 1876. Thereafter, the firm became L. F. Menage and Company, although Menage briefly took on another partner in 1878.

The depression finally lifted toward the end of the decade, and once Minneapolis entered its great boom period Menage decided to branch off into a new line of work that would eventually extend his financial reach across the United States. But before he could establish the Northwestern Guaranty Loan Company in 1884, he found himself in the middle of an enormous lawsuit that nearly bankrupted him.

~

The plaintiff in the suit was William S. King, a colorful and energetic figure who by the early 1880s had already made quite a mark in Minneapolis. He was a founder of the *Minneapolis Tribune,* a surveyor, a U.S. congressman from 1875 to 1877, an investor in the city's first street railways, and an early promoter of the Minnesota State Fair. In the late 1870s, King, who liked to attach the title of "colonel" to his name despite the inconvenient fact he had never served in the military, began staging his own annual fair on a tract of land south of Franklin

*(Above left)* William S. King, circa 1880. A wide-ranging businessman and promoter, King was the proprietor of Lyndale Farm, the largest individually owned property in the history of Minneapolis. *(Above right)* Balloon ascension at King's Fair, Minneapolis, 1881. William King staged large annual fairs between 1877 and 1882 on open grounds near Franklin Avenue and the Mississippi River. The balloon launched in 1881 made it only as far as St. Paul.

Avenue near the Mississippi River. King's Fair, as it was called, became a popular extravaganza that drew big crowds. The 1881 version included the launch of a giant hot-air balloon that was supposed to soar all the way to New York but never made it past St. Paul.

Years earlier, King had begun assembling land for a large farm south of Lake Street and east of Lakes Calhoun and Harriet. Known as Lyndale Farm, the property by 1870 encompassed fourteen hundred acres. It remains to this day the largest single piece of private property ever owned in Minneapolis. King built a house on the farm, where he raised horses and English cattle, and he also opened a resort pavilion on the shores of Lake Calhoun. But much like his balloon, King's farm did not stay aloft for long. Heavily in debt by 1875, King was on the verge of bankruptcy. His solution to this problem was the time-honored one: he borrowed more money, $120,000 in all. The lender was an old friend and financial adviser in New York named Philo Remington, who also agreed to help King sell Lyndale Farm and other properties as a way to reduce his debts.[9]

King returned to New York in the early 1880s, leaving Remington to handle his property affairs in Minneapolis. It was an arrangement King eventually came to regret. Amid much convoluted chicanery, Remington and a slippery eel of a partner named Robert Innes in 1882 struck a deal to sell off most of Lyndale Farm, more than eleven hundred acres in all. The buyer was none other than Menage, who then set about platting and developing the property in his usual manner. Among the properties Menage acquired was a resort pavilion King had built in 1877 on the northeastern shore of Lake Calhoun at West Thirty-Fifth Street. In 1883, at a cost of $200,000, Menage rebuilt the place, turning it into the Lyndale Hotel.[10]

The sprawling wood-frame hotel, which could be reached from downtown via the Minneapolis, Lyndale and Minnetonka Railway's motor line, became a favorite summer resort. On September 3, 1883, it was also the site of a spectacular feast during a day of celebration marking completion of the Northern Pacific Railroad's transcontinental line to the West Coast. The celebration attracted an impressive array of dignitaries, including President Chester A. Arthur, General (and former president) Ulysses S. Grant, General Philip Sheridan, and Northern Pacific president Henry Villard, along with the business, social, and political elite of the Twin Cities.

Following mammoth parades in St. Paul and Minneapolis, the dignitaries proceeded to the Lyndale for a late lunch. Menage had decorated the hotel with all the Victorian foofaraw he could muster and made sure his distinguished guests

(*Above top*) Lyndale Farm, 1875. William King's fourteen-hundred-acre farm, which extended between Lyndale Avenue and Lakes Calhoun and Harriet, became the focus of a hotly contested lawsuit that ended up costing Louis Menage $2 million. (*Above*) Lyndale Hotel, northeastern shore of Lake Calhoun at Thirty-Fifth Street, circa 1883. Louis Menage enlarged the resort hotel after acquiring it in 1882. Like most wooden hotels of the time, it had a short life, burning to the ground in 1888.

A Minneapolis, Lyndale and Minnetonka Railway train, near the Lyndale Hotel, circa 1880. Also known as the "Steam Motor Line," the narrow-gauge railway began operation in 1879 from downtown Minneapolis, and by 1882 extended to Excelsior on Lake Minnetonka.

would not suffer the indignity of a light meal. The menu included raw and spiced oysters, fresh lobster, broiled prairie chicken, and canvasback duck, along with such delicacies as buffalo tongue, pâté de foie gras, and orange flower ice cream. While enjoying their massive caloric intake, the assembled heavyweights were subjected to the usual round of lengthy toasts and florid speechmaking. Through it all Menage, as was his custom, seems to have kept in the background, his name nowhere mentioned in voluminous newspaper accounts of the occasion. Even so, the event offered Menage a unique opportunity to interact with the city's wealthiest and most influential citizens at a time when he was about to start what would become his signature business—the Northwestern Guaranty Loan Company.[11]

The Lyndale, unfortunately for Menage, did not prove a good investment in the long run. Like many other resort hotels of the time, its all-wood construction made it a fire waiting to happen and it burned down in 1888. Well before the hotel went up in flames, Menage had plenty of other reasons to regret his purchase of the Lyndale Farm property. The problem was that Remington and Innes,

Northern Pacific celebration and parade, Washington Avenue, Minneapolis, 1883. Completion of the railroad line to the West Coast touched off massive celebrations in Minneapolis and St. Paul. A banquet at Louis Menage's Lyndale Hotel attracted numerous dignitaries, including Ulysses S. Grant.

Menage's two partners in the deal, were schemers of the first order. Among other things, they somehow neglected to inform King of their transaction with Menage. Nor did King receive any money from the sale of his farm property. Not without reason, King began to believe he had been swindled, and he went to court.

High-priced legal talent was quickly drafted into the battle, which the local newspapers covered in considerable detail. A district court finally sided with King in 1885 after a long trial before two judges. A year later the Minnesota Supreme Court affirmed the ruling. The cost to Menage in particular was steep. He was forced to turn over about $2 million worth of property and other assets to King under the terms of the settlement. Menage later claimed, more than a little disingenuously, that he had been an innocent victim of his partners' misdeeds. But Menage, hardly a naïf in financial matters, must have known the deal was suspicious, especially since Innes had in effect demanded a kickback for his role in it.[12]

Some years later, in his voluminous *History of the City of Minneapolis,* Isaac Atwater claimed that Menage had paid off the $2 million judgment "without affecting his financial standing, scarcely ruffling his serenity." Atwater's history was a subscription book, full of glowing profiles of wealthy men who paid in advance for the privilege of being inordinately praised, and there was little truth in the account of Menage's supposed aplomb in the face of adversity. In fact, it appears the lawsuit nearly brought Menage to his knees.[13]

"Coming as it did, suddenly and unexpectedly, the lawsuit threatened bankruptcy and ruin," Menage wrote in a letter to a friend in 1895. "The history of the suit is well known to you and Minneapolis generally but not the embarrassment, headaches, and sleepless nights of those two years of disastrous litigation when it seemed as if each week would bring the ruin which was generally predicted for me." But he managed to survive the setback because by the time the supreme court issued its ruling, Menage had already established the money machine known as the Northwestern Guaranty Loan Company.[14]

～

Menage founded the company in May 1884, with offices in the newly constructed Kasota Block. Its paid-up capital, according to company documents, was $200,000. The officers included two members of Menage's family: his father-in-law, Benjamin Bull, and his younger brother, Henry. As time went on,

*"A Man of Peculiar Genius and Business Methods"*

Kasota Block, Fourth Street and Hennepin Avenue, 1886. The Northwestern Guaranty Loan Company maintained its offices here from 1884 to 1890. The building was razed in 1960 as part of the Gateway Center project.

Menage also brought in other trusted allies. Among them was William S. Streeter, who in 1889 assumed the role of Menage's second in command and who would later take on the less favorable assignment of scapegoat in chief for his boss.

In its initial form, the company dealt in mortgage loans, bonds, certificates of deposit, and so-called commercial paper (unsecured short-term notes issued to individuals). But Menage grew ever more inventive as time went on, cooking up so many schemes that by 1890 the company was at the center of a dizzying maze of interconnected businesses. A book published to commemorate the opening of the Guaranty Loan Building described the company as a model of financial probity. "Every known safeguard is thrown around the business for the protection of stockholders and investors," the book proclaimed. "Conservatism is the watchword of its officers." This does not seem to have been even remotely true.[15]

In fact, Menage and his company played fast and loose with money from the outset. After his financial empire disintegrated, there was much debate as to whether Menage had been running a criminal enterprise all along, or whether he was merely a hard-charging entrepreneur who took on too much debt and got in over his head. What's certain is that he was very creative when it came to his business methods.

After the Guaranty Loan Company collapsed, a Minneapolis banker named J. F. R. Foss told an intriguing tale to the *Minneapolis Tribune* about how Menage had actually obtained the $200,000 in capital used to start his business. According to Foss, Menage ginned up a deal whereby he sold a piece of property for $2.8 million even though its actual worth was perhaps a tenth of that amount. He then bought it back the next day for a nominal down payment, mortgaged it for $2.8 million, and used $200,000 from the proceeds as capital for his new company. As part of the scheme, Foss said, Menage then intended to issue bonds, using the mortgages as collateral. It was the equivalent of whipping up a tasty soufflé out of little but thin air.[16]

Other irregularities also became obvious as time went on. There was, for instance, the matter of the company's board of directors, which on paper included many leaders of the Minneapolis business community. Not all of these worthies, however, were aware they had been accorded the honor of serving on the board. One of them, George A. Pillsbury, was finally forced to sue Menage in 1891 to have his name removed from all company literature.[17]

When Menage's debt-ridden empire met its end, a number of Minneapolis businessmen made it clear they thought he had been a crook from the very beginning. Yet none of them seem to have voiced any concerns before the collapse occurred. The supposedly astute members of the company's board were equally reticent. They gave Menage a free hand and never challenged his activities, despite receiving well-founded complaints about how he did business.

~

One of the few images of Menage, in the form of an engraved portrait, appears in Atwater's *History of the City of Minneapolis*, published in 1893, just before the Guaranty Loan Company plunged into bankruptcy. The portrait, showing Menage when he was about forty, reveals a dapper-looking man with a high forehead, light-colored but deep-set eyes, short hair parted on the left side, and a well-tended beard. He is wearing a double-breasted jacket, the usual stiff collar, but no tie. His expression is cool and neutral, that of a man not given to revealing much about himself.

The image seems in line with what little is known about Menage's personality. Atwater, in his laudatory profile of Menage, described him as "modest and retiring in disposition, and reticent in speech. He has the faculty of inspiring confidence, and seems to possess the rare combination of boldness in conception, and caution and prudence in action." That Menage could "inspire confidence" seems evident from his remarkably fast rise as a property developer and financier, but "caution and prudence in action" would not prove to be hallmarks of his career.[18]

Perhaps the fullest picture of Menage and his personality appeared in a long story written for the *New York Herald* in September 1893, four months after the collapse of Menage's financial empire. The story, reprinted in full a few days later by the *Minneapolis Tribune,* was written by Hartley Davis, a *Herald* reporter who had once lived in Minneapolis. Davis depicted Menage as the classic plunger, a brilliant but obsessed man always looking for the next big deal. Although he delivered a devastating indictment of Menage's business practices, Davis thought the cause of Menage's downfall may have had more to do with a kind of uncontrollable optimism than any deep criminal intent.

"He was a universal optimist, an egregious egotist," Davis wrote. "His worst enemy who knows much about him will probably agree that he intended to be honest; that he had a monomania on his power of money making; that he believed he would make enough money out of his schemes to pay all of his indebtedness,

(*Above left*) Louis Menage, circa 1890. Secretive by nature, Menage rarely posed for photographs and few images of him are known to exist. (*Above right*) Page one headline from the *Minneapolis Tribune,* September 20, 1893. The stunning failure of the Northwestern Guaranty Loan Company made headlines in the Minneapolis and St. Paul newspapers as well as in New York, where many investors sustained heavy losses.

precisely as a man thinks he can gamble and win back all the money that he has taken. Menage could never understand why people would not pay five and six times what property was worth simply because he said it was worth five or six times what it was."[19]

Menage's endless financial maneuverings left little time for other activities. Even so, Davis reported that a visitor to Menage's house one night was surprised to learn that his host was on the roof with a telescope, studying the stars. "That was the first that Minneapolis knew that Menage had any ideas outside of real estate," Davis wrote. But Menage in fact was interested in sciences other than astronomy. In 1890 he pledged $10,000 to support an expedition to the Philippines in search of new species. Led by two young scientists from the University of Michigan, the expedition eventually returned with more than five thousand specimens.[20]

The Northwestern Guaranty Loan Company was hardly Menage's only enterprise. He continued his real estate business, under the name of Menage Realty Company, but also branched out into a bewildering array of other endeavors. By 1890, he had organized or taken over at least thirty-five corporations, which did business all around the country. He controlled large swaths of real estate in locations ranging from Gary, Indiana, to Galveston, Texas, to the Seattle, Washington, area. Although developing real estate remained his principal business, he also financed utilities and streetcar lines in Montana and even invested in an iron mine in Washington State.[21]

All of these ventures were massively leveraged, often by means of multiple mortgages taken out on properties with highly inflated values. Menage's dealings in Washington State, where he began acquiring undeveloped land around 1890, were typical of his operation. Among his properties in Washington was a tract of almost thirteen hundred acres just north of Seattle along the Puget Sound. Apparently intending to establish an industrial town around an iron mine and steel mill he hoped to develop nearby, Menage quickly secured multiple mortgages on the land for far more than it was worth. In one case, unimproved property he had purchased for $102,000 was later found to be mortgaged to the tune of $712,000.[22]

Yet the key to Menage's success was his ability to turn debt into cash by selling his dubious mortgages and commercial paper at a discount to eastern investors. Some of these investors were well-known figures in New York. In his story for the *New York Herald*, Hartley Davis said these investors had "absolute confidence" in Menage and the Guaranty Loan Company and could "scarcely believe" it when the company suddenly went under.[23]

In the late 1880s, however, the rot at the core of Menage's company was still well hidden from public view. As far as anyone knew, the young company was one of the city's great success stories, a financial juggernaut hurtling toward a future without limits. Menage himself undoubtedly believed in that gorgeous vision, so much so that some time in 1887 he began laying plans for a building that would show Minneapolis, and the nation, just how far his company had come in the three years since its founding.

# "One of the Great Architects of the Day"

nce he determined to erect a new home for the Northwestern Guaranty Loan Company, Louis Menage faced the difficult task of selecting an architect for the project. Perhaps the most obvious choice for the job would have been the partnership of Franklin Long and Frederick Kees. Established in 1884, Long and Kees by 1887 had designed some of Minneapolis's most prominent commercial buildings, among them the Lumber Exchange and the Kasota Block, where Menage initially had his offices. In 1888 the firm enhanced its prestige by securing one of the choicest plums of the day, winning a competition to design the gigantic new Municipal Building.[1]

But Menage instead selected E. Townsend Mix as his architect, and at first glance it was a surprising choice, since Mix had only recently moved to Minneapolis after practicing for many years in Milwaukee. Exactly how and why Menage settled on Mix is open to speculation. It is possible Menage interviewed a number of candidates and even solicited proposed designs for his new building before making his choice. The more likely scenario, however, is that Menage zeroed in

---

Lumber Exchange, Fifth Street and Hennepin Avenue, circa 1886. At ten stories, the Lumber Exchange was the tallest building in Minneapolis when it opened in 1886. Later, two stories were added and the building was extended along Hennepin. It remains the oldest high-rise in the Twin Cities.

on Mix from the start, probably at the recommendation of William D. Washburn, who served on the Guaranty Loan Company's board of directors.

A fast-moving man who in the words of one biographer "swooped through dozens of enterprises," Washburn was one of Minneapolis's wealthiest and most prominent citizens, with interests in banking, railroading, and newspaper publishing. But he was most strongly associated with the Washburn-Crosby Milling Company, which had been cofounded by one of his brothers, Cadwallader. By the time the Guaranty Loan Building began rising out of the ground, William Washburn was also a member of the U.S. Senate, where he served from 1889 to 1895.[2]

William Washburn, circa 1880. A businessman and later U.S. senator, Washburn may have been behind the decision to hire E. Townsend Mix to design the Guaranty Loan Building.

It was Washburn, in name at least, who in 1888 purchased the site for Menage's building at a cost of $210,000. In all likelihood Washburn also recommended Mix as the architect of the project. Washburn knew Mix well. In the early 1880s Mix had designed Washburn's enormous mansion just south of downtown. Washburn hired Mix to design his Gilded Age palace after first rejecting, for reasons unknown, a plan submitted by the soon-to-be celebrated New York architectural firm of McKim, Mead and White. Mix was hardly known in Minneapolis at the time, and how he came to be selected as the architect of Washburn's mansion remains a mystery.[3]

The mansion, known as "Fairoaks," was Mix's first work in Minneapolis and it must have turned quite a few heads. Completed in 1884 and demolished just forty years later, it stood near the northwest corner of the park that now bears its name, across from the Minneapolis Institute of Art (designed by McKim, Mead and White thirty years after their rebuff from Washburn). Built with walls of Kasota stone from southern Minnesota, the mansion was a rambling, high-towered, stylistically eclectic exercise in opulence set amid ten acres of beautifully landscaped grounds. By some accounts the place was worth $750,000, an astounding sum at

William Washburn Mansion, Minneapolis, just before its demolition in 1924. In the early 1880s Washburn engaged E. Townsend Mix, then based in Milwaukee, to design this enormous house at Twenty-Second Street and Stevens Avenue, where Fair Oaks Park is today. The mansion was among the largest ever built in Minneapolis.

the time, and at thirty thousand or so square feet, it was the largest mansion yet built in Minneapolis.[4]

Mix also secured another commission in Minneapolis from the Washburn family, for an orphanage built in 1886 at Fiftieth Street and Nicollet Avenue, on what is now the site of Ramsey Middle School. Known as the Washburn Memorial Orphan Asylum, the institution was founded with a bequest from Cadwallader Washburn, who died in 1882. The three-story brick building, razed in about 1930 after the orphanage closed, was a rather standard Victorian mishmash that did not rank among Mix's best work.

Mix's connections to the Washburn family undoubtedly played a vital role in his decision to relocate to Minneapolis in the late 1880s. "Fairoaks" and the orphanage provided Mix with a foothold, and he soon secured even bigger projects in the Twin Cities, culminating in the last and greatest work of his career: the Northwestern Guaranty Loan Building. When E. Townsend Mix died less than five months after the opening of the Guaranty Loan Building, the *St. Paul Daily Globe* hailed him as "one of the great architects of the day." Florid tributes to the dead were common in Victorian-era newspapers, and Mix in fact was not a renowned figure in American architecture. But he was a versatile and inventive designer who, within a span of only six years, created an exceptional group of buildings in the Twin Cities.[5]

E. Townsend Mix, date unknown. A New Englander by birth, Mix began his architectural career in Chicago in the 1850s. He soon moved to Milwaukee, where he built a highly successful practice. A series of lucrative commissions drew him to Minneapolis in the late 1880s.

Edward Townsend Mix, like many of the clients he served, hailed from an old New England family. The son and grandson of sea captains, Mix was born in New Haven, Connecticut, in 1831. He took his first name from his father and his middle name from his mother, Mary Townsend. A profile of Mix in an 1881 *History of Milwaukee* described his mother as "a woman of superior culture, great force of character and exalted virtue," and it was apparently she who provided much of his education. Mix must have been very close to her because throughout his professional career he always went by E. Townsend Mix, rather than using his first name.[6]

The family moved to Illinois in 1836 but relocated to New York ten years later. Mix showed early talent in drawing, and in 1848 he returned to New Haven to study and work with an architect there. Like most American architects of the time, Mix had no formal academic training in his chosen profession. Instead, an apprenticeship of the kind Mix undertook in New Haven was the usual path to a career in architecture.

After completing his training, Mix moved to Chicago in 1855 and went into practice with William Boyington. Best known today as the architect of the historic Chicago Water Tower (1869) on Michigan Avenue, Boyington had a large and varied practice that extended as far north as St. Paul, where he designed First Baptist Church (1875), still a landmark in the Lowertown neighborhood. Mix did not stay with Boyington for long. Obviously ambitious, he started his own practice in Milwaukee in 1857 and by 1870 had established himself as that city's preeminent architect.[7]

Not much is known about Mix's personal life. He was married to Mary Hayes, a cousin of Rutherford B. Hayes, who would later become president of the United States. The couple had no children. Like his last client, Louis Menage, Mix seems to have been a very private man. "To refer to the private or real life of Mr. Mix is as if entering on forbidden ground," wrote one chronicler of Milwaukee in 1895, five years after Mix's death. "He was singularly reticent as regards his own personal characteristics, a gentleman in the finest sense of the word."[8]

Although Milwaukee eventually became known for its breweries and large German population, most of the city's early settlers were from New York and New England, and it was from this group that Mix drew the bulk of his clientele. As a designer, Mix for the most part followed the prevailing styles of the day. One of his landmarks in Milwaukee is the French Second Empire–style Mitchell Building (1876), an ornate six-story office structure complete with a mansarded dome. Toward the end of his career in Milwaukee he produced perhaps his finest work there, the Chamber of Commerce (now Mackie) Building, completed in 1880. An elusive blend of English and Italian influences, the building bristles with odd and striking details. Nine years later, Mix's Guaranty Loan Building would also display many distinctive features.

Mix's career in Milwaukee went into decline by the late 1870s, when the city's German community began dominating the business and political landscape. As the city's old-line Yankees lost influence, so did Mix. In 1878 he engaged in a bitterly fought competition with a German-born architect to win the lucrative commission for a large new county insane asylum. He lost the job and later called the competition "a farce." Mix's health at this time was also in decline. He was afflicted with tuberculosis, and in 1879 he suffered a severe attack of pneumonia from which he never fully recovered.[9]

With his commissions in Milwaukee drying up, Mix began to look for busi-

Chamber of Commerce (Mackie) Building, Milwaukee, circa 1950s. Completed in 1880, the Mackie Building is considered one of E. Townsend Mix's finest works, with many vivid and striking details. It still stands in downtown Milwaukee.

———————

ness elsewhere. It's not clear exactly when he relocated to Minneapolis, but his name first appears in city directories in 1888–89, when he is listed as living at the West Hotel with his wife. After resettling in Minneapolis, Mix took on a partner, Walter A. Holbrook, about whom little is known. Mix also began advertising his services on a regular basis in both the *Minneapolis Tribune* and *St. Paul Daily Globe*.

Once he had made the connection with the Washburns, Mix found the Twin Cities to be fertile ground. Between 1886 and 1888 he secured commissions for three large office buildings, including one in downtown St. Paul, before taking on his ultimate project for Menage. All of these predecessors to the Guaranty Loan Building were organized around interior light courts, or atriums, an arrangement Mix clearly preferred above all others. Light courts were a distinctive feature of many of the first generation of tall office buildings in the United States. Soaring to unprecedented heights, these buildings soon became known as skyscrapers.

∼

Skyscrapers were an American invention. Two cities—New York and Chicago—were at the forefront of their development, although smaller cities like Minneapolis and St. Paul quickly adopted the new building type. In New York, the first commercial building that might fairly be called a skyscraper was the eight-story Equitable Building, completed in 1870. It featured an interior frame of cast and wrought iron and two steam-powered Otis elevators. Even so, the building's exterior walls were of traditional masonry construction in the form of massive blocks of stone. This sort of composite structural system for skyscrapers would continue in widespread use right up to the time of the Guaranty Loan Building.[10]

As a new building type, skyscrapers presented daunting aesthetic and practical problems for architects. The Chicago architect Louis Sullivan, who famously wrote that a skyscraper "must be every inch a proud and soaring thing," resolved many of the aesthetic issues in such seminal works as the Wainwright Building (1890) in St. Louis. But the practical issues presented by skyscrapers (how to provide fast and reliable elevator service, how to make plumbing and heating work, how to fireproof metal frames) were equally challenging. One of the greatest problems was light.[11]

Although electric lighting, using a direct current system pioneered by Thomas Edison, was available by the 1880s, it was not considered adequate to illuminate the interiors of large office buildings such as the Guaranty Loan. As a result, good daylighting remained essential. But with clients wanting ever bigger and taller office buildings, architects struggled with how to bring enough natural light into interior offices. It was a crucial issue because the better architects were able to command light, the more desirable and therefore rentable office spaces became.

In New York, where lots tended to be small, architects early on favored slender, tower-like buildings that provided ample daylight for offices. But as building footprints grew larger, architects turned to more complex forms to ensure adequate light. U-shaped, E-shaped, and H-shaped buildings were among the most common configurations, and they made it possible to design very large buildings in which every office would have windows to the outside. In Chicago, where downtown lots tended to be larger than in Manhattan, architects discovered that another efficient option was the hollow square, with offices surrounding a central light court.[12]

There were two basic types of light court buildings. One approach was to hollow out the building but leave most of the central court open to the elements above a one- or two-story skylit lobby. The second approach, as exemplified by the Guaranty Loan Building, was to enclose the entire light court by means of a rooftop skylight.

Most of the best American examples of full-height light court buildings date to the 1880s and 1890s. Perhaps the most spectacular of them all was the twenty-one-story Masonic Temple, the tallest building in the world when it was completed in Chicago in 1892. At its center was a twenty-story, 308-foot central

Germania Life (later Guardian) Building, Fourth and Minnesota Streets, St. Paul, circa 1905. Completed in 1889, the U-shaped building was designed so that daylight could penetrate into all the offices. It was demolished in 1970.

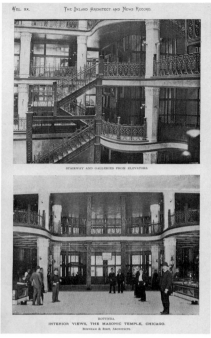

(*Above left*) Masonic Temple, Chicago, circa 1900. Rising twenty-one stories, the Masonic Temple was the world's tallest building when it opened in 1892. Its offices, like those in the Guaranty Loan Building, were organized around a huge court set beneath a skylight. (*Above right*) Light court, Masonic Temple, Chicago, 1892. Twenty floors of offices and shops looked out over the court, which when built was the tallest of its kind in the world

light court ringed by offices, shops, and Masonic meeting rooms. Designed by the celebrated Chicago architectural firm of Burnham and Root, the building, despite its stunning atrium, was never a financial success owing to a variety of functional shortcomings and was torn down in 1939.[13]

In the Twin Cities alone, forty or more downtown buildings constructed between 1880 and 1900 included a central light court of one kind or another. Almost all are gone. The largest and most spectacular skylit courts were incorporated into office and public buildings, but they also could be found in hotels, department stores, and apartment buildings. Only scant descriptions and few, if any, images exist for many of these light courts, which were such a routine architectural feature that they rarely attracted comment.[14]

Corridor with vaulted skylight, New York Life Insurance Building, Sixth and Minnesota Streets, St. Paul, circa 1908. Unlike the Guaranty Loan Building, the New York Life had a light court open to the elements, leaving room below for a long, skylit corridor leading to the lobby. Built in 1889, the New York Life fell to the wrecker in 1967.

Fittingly enough, one of Mix's works, Temple Court, was very probably the first tall office building in the Twin Cities with a full-height, enclosed light court. The eight-story building opened in 1886 at the corner of Hennepin and Washington Avenues. It was built on the site of the city's largest pioneer-era theater, the Academy of Music, which burned down on Christmas Day 1884.[15]

Real estate and streetcar magnate Thomas Lowry, one of the theater's owners, led the way in developing Temple Court and presumably played a key role in hiring Mix for the project. Lowry, as it happened, was also an active and influential

Academy of Music, Hennepin and Washington Avenues, after fire, 1884. The fire broke out on Christmas Day and quickly destroyed the thirteen-hundred-seat theater. Temple Court, an eight-story office building designed by E. Townsend Mix, opened on the site two years later.

---

member of the Northwestern Guaranty Loan Company's board of directors and later the firm's vice president. Mix's relationship with Lowry, like his connections to the Washburns, may well have helped him win the commission for the Guaranty Loan Building.

A straightforward brick structure with few stylistic flourishes, Temple Court had about 250 offices, many occupied by lawyers. Two open-cage elevators lifted tenants to the upper floors. The 30-by-60-foot light court in the middle of the building was surrounded by galleries that provided access to all the offices. A central bridge spanned the court at every floor to provide access to the elevators. This was an unusual arrangement not found in any of Mix's other office buildings. No interior photographs of Temple Court have been found, but it is known that the galleries had translucent glass floors similar to those Mix later specified for the Guaranty Loan Building. Later known as the Gateway Building, Temple Court was razed in 1953, five years before the Gateway Center urban renewal project was under way.

Following the completion of Temple Court, five more tall office buildings with enclosed light courts, including three designed by Mix, were constructed in the Twin Cities between 1887 and 1890. One of the most conspicuous was the Boston Block at Third Street and Hennepin Avenue. Built in 1881, possibly with a small, enclosed light court, the Boston Block underwent extension reconstruction after a fire in 1886 heavily damaged the upper floors. As part of the work, completed in early 1887, architect Leroy Buffington added two floors to the building, raising it to seven stories. He also carved out a new 45-by-80-foot central light court beneath

(*Above*) Boston Block, Third Street and Hennepin Avenue, circa 1892. A fire caused extensive damage to the building in 1886. It was promptly rebuilt with two additional stories and a new light court. (*Opposite*) Temple Court, Hennepin and Washington Avenues, circa 1890. The building, which stood until 1953, featured a light court with glass-floored galleries similar to those in the Guaranty Loan Building.

what was claimed to be the "largest double skylight in the Northwest." The court was nearly as large as the one that would soon grace the Guaranty Loan Building.[16]

A drawing from Buffington's office provides the only known image of the Boston Block's light court, which apparently remained more or less intact until the building was demolished in 1942–43. Although it offers only a partial view, the drawing depicts two open-cage (and largely unscreened) elevators, decorative iron railings, tiled gallery floors, and offices with large windows facing toward the court. If the drawing shows the court as it was actually built, it must have been the finest space of its kind in the Twin Cities before the Guaranty Loan Building rose a few blocks to the east on Third Street.

Mix, meanwhile, was busy with two new office buildings for the *Globe* newspaper, which in the 1880s published daily editions in St. Paul and Minneapolis. Both buildings featured full-height but very compact light courts. The first of the Globe buildings was completed at Fourth and Cedar Streets in St. Paul in 1887. At ten stories, it was for a brief period the tallest building in the city. Its light court, only about eighteen feet square, was served by two elevators. The building as a whole was highly eclectic in style and included a corner lookout tower, a feature Mix would employ again for the Guaranty Loan Building. The Globe Building came down in 1959, one of hundreds of old buildings that fell to the wrecker in downtown St. Paul during the urban renewal era.[17]

The Globe Building's reign atop the St. Paul skyline lasted only two years.

Light court, Boston Block, Minneapolis, 1881. Measuring 45 by 80 feet, the light court was the largest in Minneapolis until the Guaranty Loan Building opened three years later. The Boston Block was razed in 1942–43, well before the Gateway Center project claimed most of the buildings around it.

Stung by its competitor's highly visible achievement, the *St. Paul Pioneer Press* quickly hired Chicago architect Solon Beman to design a twelve-story building (later expanded to sixteen stories) at Fourth and Robert Streets. Completed in 1889, the Pioneer Building, which has an enclosed central light court, still stands and was converted into apartments in 2014. The Pioneer's sixteen-story light court is the only one of its era left in the Twin Cities and one of very few remaining in the United States.[18]

Mix's second building for the *Globe*, in Minneapolis, was completed in 1889 at 220–24 Fourth Street South, between Hennepin and Nicollet Avenues. Eight stories high and faced in rusticated red sandstone, the building was long and narrow, with only forty-four feet of frontage along Fourth. Even so, it included a small central light court, about 16 by 20 feet, beneath the usual rooftop skylight. An angled corner tower crowned by a witch's-hat roof was the building's most memorable feature. Some of the building's rather quirky detailing, such as

Globe Building, Fourth and Cedar Streets, St. Paul, circa 1902. This ten-story building topped the St. Paul skyline when it opened in 1887. Built for the *St. Paul Daily Globe*, it was demolished in 1959.

Light court, Pioneer Building, Fourth and Robert Streets, St. Paul, 2015. The sixteen-story light court is one of the last of its era in the United States. The building, most of which dates to 1889, has been converted to apartments.

chimney-like vertical elements flanking the tower, would reappear on the Guaranty Loan, which Mix was designing at the same time. The Globe Building and all the others on its block were razed in 1958 to make way for a new Minneapolis central library that opened in 1961.[19]

As work began on the Guaranty Loan Building in 1888, the new U.S. Post Office and Federal Court Building was nearing completion immediately to its west on the same block. Designed like all federal buildings of the time by the supervising architect of the U.S. Treasury, the post office was a gawky mélange of classical elements faced in white Ohio sandstone. Originally three-and-a-half stories high and later expanded to a full four, it included a 152-foot clock tower along Third Street and a pair of smaller towers overlooking Marquette Avenue. Despite its pretensions to grandeur, the new post office seems to have been misbegotten from the start. One writer complained that the federal government's "very meagre appropriations" for the building simply left it too small for its intended purpose.[20]

Globe Building, Fourth Street between Hennepin and Nicollet Avenues, circa 1895. The most picturesque of E. Townsend Mix's skyscrapers, the Globe opened in 1889. It was razed in 1958 to make way for a new central library that is now gone as well.

U.S. Post Office, Third Street and Marquette Avenue, circa 1908. A rather clumsy exercise in classicism, the building opened in 1889 just as the Guaranty Loan Building was nearing completion next door. The old post office came down, with little fanfare, in 1961.

———————————

St. Paul, by contrast, would complete the first stage of a far more admired U.S. post office in 1892. That building, now Landmark Center, was on a larger and more attractive site than its Minneapolis counterpart, and its architecture was of a higher quality. Yet the much maligned Minneapolis building, which was used as a post office for only twenty-six years, did share one feature with Landmark Center—a skylit central court. Given how poorly regarded the old post office was, it is hardly surprising that the press and public took little notice when it was torn down in 1961 just months before its famous neighbor also fell to the wrecker.

~

Construction of the Guaranty Loan Building started in May 1888 after a foundation permit was issued by the city. Mix by this time had hired Charles Ferrin, a carpenter turned architect, to supervise the project. The work seems to have gone smoothly, although it required about six months of work to complete the massive 12-by-15-foot stone piers needed to support such a large and heavy building. The piers were built of granite from Ortonville, Minnesota, the same stone that would soon be used to construct the walls of the huge new Municipal Building a few blocks away. A full building permit for the Guaranty Loan was issued on December 7, 1888. The permit was for $250,000, far less than what the building actually cost. There was apparently a cornerstone-laying ceremony at about the same time, but it does not seem to have been noted in the local press. Meanwhile, the *Minneapolis*

*Tribune* reported that work on the building's walls would proceed through the winter, with the mortar being heated in furnaces "so that when the stones are laid it will dry out before freezing."[21]

By February 1889, the *Saturday Evening Spectator*, a weekly newspaper in Minneapolis, reported that "the first story is nearly up of the mammoth twelve story building now under construction on the corner of Third street and Second avenue south for the Northwestern Guaranty Loan company." Other local newspapers also issued brief progress reports. The construction contract for the building specified that its lower three floors, built of granite, were to be completed by June 1889 and that the building was to be fully enclosed by December of that year. It appears the general contractor for the project, Horace N. Leighton and Company of Minneapolis, met these deadlines.[22]

The Leighton Company was one of the city's largest contracting firms. Its founder, Horace N. Leighton, like so many people associated with the building, was a transplanted New Englander. Born in Maine, he arrived in Minneapolis in about 1875, found work as a carpenter and then went into business for himself. Three brothers were also part of the firm, which would go on to build other major Minneapolis monuments, including the Basilica of Saint Mary.[23]

Menage undoubtedly stayed well informed about the work on his building. In a newspaper account of the grand opening in 1890, he talked at some length about the building's heating system, suggesting that he had kept a close eye on every detail of the project. Yet even as his mighty dream of a building took shape, Menage had to cope with an unexpected family tragedy.[24] His younger brother, Henry G. Menage, had joined him in the real estate business in Minneapolis in the late 1870s. He later became treasurer of the Northwestern Guaranty Loan Company, although real estate seems to have been his principal occupation. At the end of July 1889, Henry Menage became seriously ill with erysipelas, an acute bacterial infection that often proved fatal before the age of antibiotics. A week after contracting the infection, Henry Menage died, at age thirty-seven, at his brother's apartment on Eighth Street.[25]

Only three months later, in November, Louis Menage lost another family member when his father-in-law, Benjamin S. Bull, died at age fifty-seven. Bull had also been active in the Guaranty Loan Company. It's not known how these deaths affected Menage, but there is no evidence that they caused him to slow the frenetic pace of his business activity.[26]

There was also at this time a small but, as it turned out, prophetic cloud on Menage's horizon. Sometime in 1889 a Minneapolis real estate dealer named John H. Burke began to take an interest in the Northwestern Guaranty Loan Company. Burke, who had once been a bank examiner, nosed around real estate records at the county courthouse and analyzed financial statements on file with the state. He didn't like what he saw. Suspecting that Menage was in effect stealing from his own company, Burke started to raise uncomfortable questions. His early attempt to bring his concerns to light failed, but within a year he would make explosive allegations that went all the way to the company's board of directors and that later caught the attention of the press and state regulators.

Yet as Menage prepared for the grand opening of the Guaranty Loan Building on May 31, 1890, Burke remained a minor irritant. With his business apparently booming, Menage was ready to stage a spectacular event that would long be remembered as one of the greatest of its kind in the city's history.

# "The Best Office Building in the World"

On the night of Saturday, May 31, 1890, thousands of invited guests streamed into the Northwestern Guaranty Loan Building for a grand opening of such pomp and splendor that one newspaper described it as "little less than magical." Although the building by then had been open for several weeks, attracting large numbers of curious visitors, the formal reception—which followed an afternoon event open to the general public—was Louis Menage's chance to show off his mighty new edifice to the business, social, and political elite of the Twin Cities. Decked out with banners, bunting, and flowers amid the glow of multicolored limelights and thousands of incandescent bulbs, the building must indeed have seemed a magical place.[1]

All the major dailies in the Twin Cities devoted pages of gushing prose to the event. A *Minneapolis Journal* reporter, who must have been paid by the adjective, launched into an especially perfervid paean: "Today, in this most wondrous quarter of the continent, this marvellous Northwest, an event transpires of unusual importance, an event fraught with immeasurable significance. . . . Here, in a comparatively young city . . . where but yesterday the sturdy pioneer blew from his bugle the clear clarion notes that told of the oncoming advance of him and

Guaranty Loan Building, circa 1900. This early photograph was taken from the top floor or roof of Harmonia Hall, a four-story building that stood kitty-corner from the Guaranty Loan at Third Street and Second Avenue South.

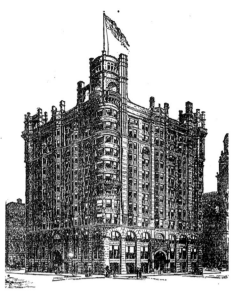

**MINNEAPOLIS.**

**ALL ARE PROUD OF IT.**

The Guaranty Loan Building Henceforth the Pride of the City of Minneapolis.

The Reception Yesterday One of the Most Successful Events in Local History.

Description of a Structure Without a Rival Among the Office Buildings of the World.

Prominent People in Attendance and Brief Mention of Some of the Tenants.

The *St. Paul and Minneapolis Pioneer Press* and other local newspapers gave extensive coverage to the grand opening of the Northwestern Guaranty Loan Building on May 31, 1890. "The great pile is magnificent," the *Pioneer Press* reported in a story that included a list of all the dignitaries who attended the event.

his noble fellows . . . here there has been erected a stately pile, distinctive in its nature, the most magnificent office building in the whole wide world."[2]

This overripe prose was not without a measure of truth. The building was indeed remarkable, and its grand opening, which required months of planning, was one of those glittering occasions people would remember for years. "Taking it all in," said the *Minneapolis Tribune*, "it was the greatest event of its kind that Minneapolis has ever seen, and perhaps to few in this generation will it be given to see another like it."[3]

It's not known how many invitations were issued for the evening reception, but by one estimate eight thousand people showed up. The crowd was so large that the building's main entrance on Third Street became a thick scrum of well-dressed visitors trying to elbow their way inside. "As early as 7 o'clock, the throngs began to converge toward the building," the *St. Paul and Minneapolis Pioneer Press* reported. "Every street in the city seemed to lead to it. . . . Motors, electric cars, street cars, steam cars and hacks deposited their loads before the marble entrance, and the building began to fill up. Till nearly ten the crush at the entrance continued."[4]

Once inside, visitors were greeted by Oscar Ringwall's band, one of four stationed around the building, as well as a reception committee that included such luminaries as Minnesota governor William Merriam and Minneapolis mayor Edward C. Babb. Joining the politicians on the committee were some of the city's leading businessmen, among them William Washburn, Thomas Lowry, and Charles A. Pillsbury, all members of the Guaranty Loan Company's board of directors. Curiously, Menage himself does not seem to have been among the group of greeters, and no newspaper accounts of the event made note of his presence.

Climbing up to the second floor, visitors saw for the first time the full extent of the light court, which, according to the *Tribune,* was "beautifully decorated with palms and flowers, the flash of marble and brass, throwing out the bright reflections of myriad calcium and incandescent lights . . . a sea of color such as could be looked for in a picture of a fairyland." Elevators whisked visitors to the upper floors, where many tenants opened their offices for tours. Meanwhile, uniformed waiters cruised the glass-floored galleries offering light refreshments in the form of "punch and ices." Many guests eventually made their way to rooms set aside on the third and eleventh floors for dancing to a program of waltzes, polkas, and galops.[5]

After their exertions, dancers could ascend to the rooftop garden to view the skyline and the stars from the tallest structure yet built in Minneapolis. "From the roof . . . a glorious vision was spread out below," the *Pioneer Press* wrote. "The lights of the city looked like diminutive fire flies, while the buildings in the semi-obscurity had quite the appearance of doll houses, so dwarfed were they by distance and the comparison with the great pile looming up above them." The *Tribune* was even more effusive. To reach the roof garden, the newspaper declared, "was like entering paradise. The fresh odor of the flowers and the stirring breeze was a great relief from the heat and jam [of people] below."[6]

The reception ended at eleven o'clock, and as the last guests left many of them would have passed by a large banner they had first seen above the staircase leading up to the second floor. Displayed next to a huge American flag, the banner proclaimed, "Welcome to the Best Office Building in the World." Perhaps this bold superlative was an exaggeration, but if so not by much.

∼

Observation tower, Guaranty Loan Building, circa 1890. The tower stood 222 feet above the street and attracted thousands of visitors, who paid a quarter to take in the scenery. The building remained the tallest in Minneapolis until 1914.

*"The Best Office Building in the World"*

The *Pioneer Press* published a lengthy list of local luminaries who attended the grand opening. One name—that of E. Townsend Mix—was notably absent from the list, and it's possible the man who created the greatest building yet seen in Minneapolis was not on hand to witnesses the spectacle of its formal unveiling. Nor did Mix receive much notice in the press for his work. Several newspapers provided lengthy descriptions of the "wonderful building," as it was repeatedly called, without bothering to mention Mix. Only the *Tribune*, at the very end of its story, saluted Mix for his design, saying the building was "worthy of his genius."

If Mix did not attend the grand opening, it may be because he was a dying man. Afflicted with tuberculosis, he grew increasingly ill during the summer of 1890. Even so, he kept on working, having secured a commission from Thomas Lowry for a large project in downtown St. Paul known as the Lowry Arcade Building. But his condition steadily worsened, and on September 23 he died at age fifty-nine in his rooms at the West Hotel. An obituary in the *St. Paul Daily Globe*, for whom Mix designed two office buildings, said that although "he had been very feeble" he was still "attending to the details for the completion of the Arcade building" just two days before his death. A briefer obituary in the *Tribune* concluded by noting that "his latest achievement, the Northwestern Guaranty Loan Building . . . will stand as a monument to his memory."[7]

Although Mix left behind a rich body of work in both Milwaukee and the Twin Cities, the Guaranty Loan was his unquestioned masterpiece. From his windows at the West, Mix would have been able to see it, the largest and most stunning edifice on the Minneapolis skyline, and the mighty building must have been a source of pride for him as his life slowly slipped away.

Louis Menage also took great pride in the Guaranty Loan, and on the day of the grand opening, he gave a rare interview, to the *Minneapolis Journal*, in which he talked at some length about the building. "We determined from the outset that everything about this building should be of the very best," he said, before launching into a surprisingly detailed description of the "non-explosive" boiler in the basement. "I mention this," he went on to say, "to show you that in a building like this we could not afford to and would not have anything that should not be first-class. There is not another such building as this in the world. When we say this we mean it."[8]

Menage's claim to his building's absolute superiority might well have produced skepticism in New York and Chicago, where bigger and higher office

New York Life Insurance Building, Fifth Street and Second Avenue South, 1911. Built in 1890 and demolished in 1958, the ten-story building offered a suavely classical look that was much different from the Guaranty Loan's rather rough, rugged appearance.

*"The Best Office Building in the World"*

Corner of the Guaranty Loan Building (renamed the Metropolitan in 1905) at Third Street and Second Avenue South, 1959. Massive blocks of New Hampshire granite formed the building's three-story base.

buildings were already in existence. Even so, Menage's remarks were not pure puffery. The Guaranty Loan did indeed stand in the first rank of American office buildings of its era by virtue of its overall quality, magnificent light court, and state-of-the-art amenities. In Minneapolis it had no peer. With a frontage of 156 feet on Second Avenue South and 132 feet on Third Street, and with its corner tower reaching well over 200 feet above the street, it was the city's largest and tallest office building.[9]

It was also an odd building in many ways, beginning with its almost fiercely old-fashioned appearance. The building's craggy stone walls and rooftop towers looked back to medieval castles rather than toward the modernist future evident in the clean, relatively unadorned lines of many Chicago skyscrapers of the period. The Guaranty Loan's primitive-looking exterior was in sharp contrast to that of another large new office building, for the New York Life Insurance Company, completed a month earlier only two blocks away at Fifth Street and Second Avenue South. Designed by a New York architectural firm, the ten-story building was a sedate exercise in the up-and-coming Renaissance Revival style that would have been at home in Manhattan. The Guaranty Loan, on the other hand, would have struck most observers as a rude interloper amid New York's well-mannered skyscrapers.[10]

∿

The Guaranty Loan's imposing stone walls were not merely for show, as is the case with most modern skyscrapers, which typically feature a thin skin of stone, brick, glass, or some other material wrapped around a steel or concrete frame. Four feet thick at the base and then tapering to about two feet on the upper floors, the outer stone walls of the Guaranty Loan were integral to its structure, not only supporting themselves but also anchoring the iron-and-steel frame within the building. This sort of composite structural system was common until the early 1890s, when entirely steel-framed skyscrapers became the norm. High, thick stone walls of the type used for the Guaranty Loan could be prone to settling over time, causing any number of problems, but that never occurred—a testament to the strength and solidity of the building's foundations.

The building's interior frame consisted of cast-iron columns and a mix of wrought-iron and steel beams, all bolted together. As was the usual practice, virtually all the framing was encased in fire-resistant terra-cotta tile, since exposed metal will deform at relatively low temperatures in a fire. Floors and fixed interior walls were built using the same type of tile. Some brick was also used for backing walls. Part of what made the building so remarkable was the visibility of its interior structure. Columns, beams, joints, and fittings were exposed in many places, especially around the light court, so that visitors could actually see how the building was put together.[11]

Because of how it was built, the Guaranty Loan was routinely advertised as "fireproof." This wasn't strictly true; furnishings and other contents could certainly have burned. Much later, as the building faced the prospect of demolition, city officials would claim that it was in fact a fire hazard, primarily because of its central court (which could act as a flue for smoke and flames), its unprotected elevators, and its open staircases. Yet during the seventy-two years it stood, the

company used for floor arches constitute the greatest strength with the

: and mate-

e-third the

oncrete

a level

voiding

ing or

icularly

l1vid-

of a

)art-

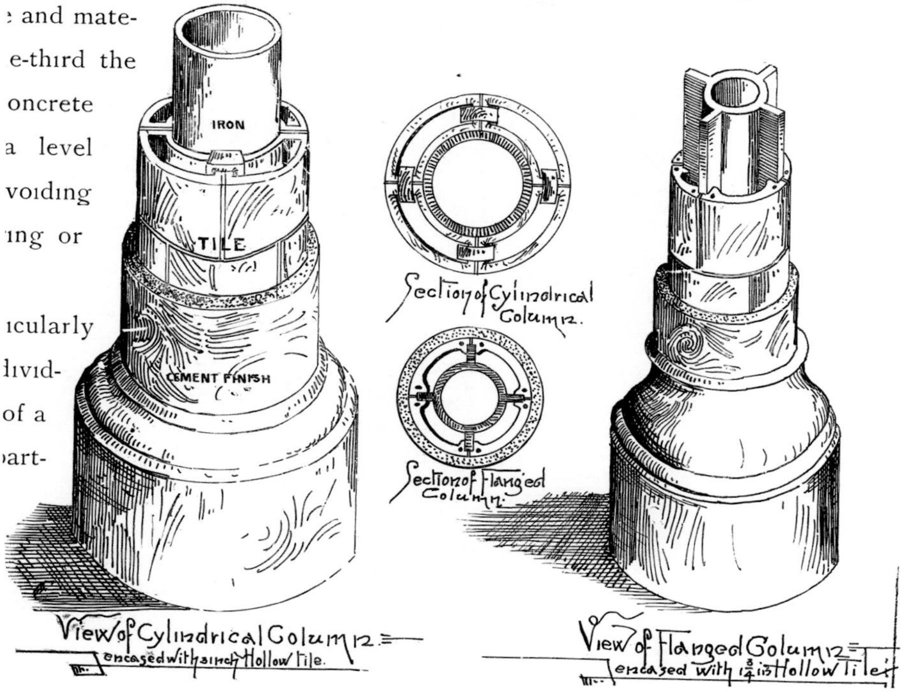

The Guaranty Loan Building's interior iron columns were encased in tile to protect against fire. During its seventy-two years, the building never experienced a fire of any consequence.

building never experienced a serious fire or any major structural problems. As Menage had said just before the grand opening, everything about the building truly was "first-class."

~

Although the Guaranty Loan garnered no shortage of praise from the press when it opened, not everyone was impressed by its rough, rockbound exterior. The architectural critic Montgomery Schuyler, who favored quiet classicism, wrote in 1891 that the Guaranty Loan "has many striking details not without ingenuity . . . but as certainly without the refinement that comes of a studied and affectionate elaboration."[12]

Second floor, Metropolitan Building, 1960. The lower levels of the building featured custom-designed glass-block flooring that allowed light to penetrate deep into the structure.

Cass Gilbert, who in 1895 would win a competition to design the Minnesota State Capitol and then go on to a national career, was another early critic. An advocate for Classical Revival styles, Gilbert found Mix's dark, towering creation to be "appalling." In his diary Gilbert wrote, "It has a great effect on the mind from its size, both inside and out but the design throughout is stupid and in bad taste, either too heavy or too light with a remarkable totality that is almost miraculous." Yet his use of the phrase "almost miraculous" at the end suggests that he, like so many others who experienced the building, found something undeniably compelling about it.[13]

It's not known why Mix, presumably with Menage's approval or possibly even at his behest, created such a rugged exterior for the Guaranty Loan, but the general style he chose—now known as Richardsonian Romanesque—was certainly fashionable at the time. The style takes its name from the work of Henry Hobson Richardson (1838–1886), a Boston architect who, beginning in the 1870s, created a series of massive masonry buildings derived from the eleventh- and twelfth-century Romanesque architecture of Europe. In Minnesota the style was very popular in the late 1880s and early 1890s for commercial buildings, schools, courthouses, and mansions. Minneapolis City Hall, which was started in 1889 but not completed until 1906, remains one of the state's outstanding examples of the style.

The Guaranty Loan was far from textbook Richardsonian Romanesque. Its facades were busier than those typically produced by Richardson, especially in his later works. Yet the building was distinctive and it packed an undeniable visual punch. There was nothing else like it on the Minneapolis skyline, nor did it closely resemble any other skyscraper of its time in the United States.

The building's two-tone color scheme was particularly striking. For the walls of the building, Mix selected two stones—green granite from North Conway, New Hampshire, and reddish brown Lake Superior sandstone from Portage Entry, Michigan. The granite, used for the lower three floors, was an unusual choice, particularly since high-quality Minnesota granites were readily available from the St. Cloud area and from quarries in the southwestern part of the state. But Mix clearly had a color scheme in mind when he designed the building, and he had to look outside Minnesota for the exact granite he wanted.

The New Hampshire granite Mix chose was quite new to the market. The quarry from which it came, operated by the Maine and New Hampshire

Municipal Building (Minneapolis City Hall), south across the intersection of Fourth Street and Third Avenue South, 1898. The building's powerful style, known as Richardsonian Romanesque, was very popular in the late nineteenth century. E. Townsend Mix adapted the style for the Guaranty Loan Building.

Granite Company, had opened in 1886, producing both red and green granite. The four-foot-thick blocks required for the Guaranty Loan Building would have represented a very large order for the company. It may also have been the only order the company ever received from Minnesota, given the ready supply of granites from within the state.[14]

The sandstone used for the upper nine floors of the Guaranty Loan, and for its lookouts and towers, was quarried near Lake Superior on Michigan's Keweenaw Peninsula. Sandstone quarries had been established along the southern shore of the lake in Wisconsin and Michigan as early as the 1860s, but large-scale operations didn't begin until the 1870s. The Portage Entry quarries from which the Guaranty Loan's stone came were more recent, having opened in 1883.

Lake Superior sandstone, mostly from the Keweenaw Peninsula or the Bayfield area in Wisconsin, was widely used in the Twin Cities. Strong and durable, yet easily carved, the stone, predominantly reddish brown in color, achieved its greatest popularity in the late 1880s. A good many buildings constructed with Lake Superior sandstone still stand in the Twin Cities, including the richly colored Germania Bank (now St. Paul) Building (1889) at Fifth and Wabasha Streets in downtown St. Paul.[15]

Both the granite and sandstone used for the Guaranty Loan Building were rock-faced. This meant that the face of each block of stone was left much as it came out of the quarry, with little finishing work. Rock-faced stone was less costly than the smooth, finely dressed ashlar stone often used for buildings. Given the unusually large amount of stone needed for the Guaranty Loan, Mix's choice of the rock-faced style may well have been dictated by cost considerations.

Unlike most large office structures of its time, the Guaranty Loan featured stone walls on all four sides. Normally, stone was used only for the street side of office buildings, or for two sides if the building occupied a corner. The other, less visible walls were generally finished in brick, which was cheaper than stone. But the Guaranty Loan's quarter-block site was such that all four sides of the building—not just those facing Third Street and Second Avenue South—were quite visible. On the south side, a twenty-foot-wide alley separated the Guaranty Loan from a cluster of small buildings, while on the west side it was fifty feet away from the new U.S. Post Office at Third and Marquette. Menage clearly wanted his new building to stand out in every way, and finishing it entirely in stone enhanced its monumental presence.

(*Above*) Advertisement for Portage sandstone, with a drawing of the Guaranty Loan Building, 1892. The brownish-red sandstone, quarried on Michigan's Upper Peninsula, was used for all the building's outer walls above the third floor. (*Right*) Rear of the Metropolitan Building, facing Fourth Street, 1961. This rarely seen side of the building, which originally overlooked a narrow alley, did not come into full view until other buildings on the block were demolished in the late 1950s and replaced by the new U.S. Courthouse, at left.

*"The Best Office Building in the World"*

Like many other large office buildings of its era, the Guaranty Loan was not especially grand on the ground floor, much of which was reserved for a dozen or so small shops and offices with individual entrances. There were, however, two elaborate entries to the building, one on Second and the other on Third. Although very similar in style, the two were slightly different because a small hill along Second caused the entrance there to be a foot or so above the one on Third. To even things out, Mix elongated the main entrance on Third, a subtle touch most visitors probably never noticed. Flanked by polished granite columns, the two-story arched entries included carved surrounds in a variety of botanical and geometric patterns. There was also a distinctive carved stone banner above the Second Avenue entrance. A third, less ornate entrance was located on the west side of the building, in the courtyard facing the post office.

The building's tallest floor was actually the second, which was designed to accommodate three large banking halls. This was a typical arrangement at the time and for many years to come. The second floor appealed to major commercial tenants because it was buffered from the noise and dust of the streets, as well as from the fragrant aroma of horse manure, yet remained easily accessible to the general public.

The granite portion of the Guaranty Loan ended with an arcaded third floor. The arched windows on this floor included a delightful feature—small stained-glass roundels that could be tilted open to provide ventilation. So well constructed was the building that these little round windows were still functioning quite nicely until the very end.

The upper nine stories, all in sandstone except for polished granite columns between some of the windows, were lively and varied. Tall tiers of bay windows animated all four sides of the building, starting at the fourth floor and extending to the eleventh or, in a few cases, twelfth floor. The Guaranty Loan made more extensive use of these light-capturing bays than any other office building in the Twin Cities. The main corner of the building, overlooking Second Avenue South and Third Street, featured a prominent rounded bay that extended all the way to the roof and then continued upward in the form of a fifty-foot lookout tower thrust forward on massive brackets. Halfway up the corner bay, on the sixth floor, a bracketed balcony added yet another picturesque touch to Mix's design.

Except for some arched windows on the tenth floor, where Menage had his luxurious offices, all the windows on the upper part of the building were standard

Metropolitan Building from Third Street, with the ruins of the old U.S. Post Office in the foreground, 1961. Bay windows and rough-faced stonework gave the Metropolitan an almost primitive, castle-like appearance.

wood-frame double hungs, typically arranged in pairs unless they were part of a bay. The spandrels beneath the windows were far from standard, however. Formed from long, stepped-up blocks of stone, the spandrels were unlike anything else Mix had done before and they added a cascading sense of rhythm to the building's facades.

There was also plenty of visual excitement along the building's roofline, which included lookouts at every corner, clustered chimneys, and a heavy stone parapet that doubled as a protective railing for patrons of the rooftop garden. The

Rooftop of the Metropolitan Building, showing observation tower, chimneys, and sandstone parapets, 1959. The tower and rooftop gardens had been closed for many years by the time this photograph was taken.

———————

big corner observation tower was open at the base, where a spiral staircase led up to a viewing platform 222 feet above the street. The view cost a quarter and was a popular attraction, particularly during the early years of the building when it dominated the skyline.

~

Shortly after the Guaranty Loan Building opened, it was memorialized in a handsomely illustrated book detailing every aspect of its construction and appearance. Called simply *The Northwestern Guaranty Loan Company's Building,* the book is a rare item, with the University of Minnesota Libraries holding one of the few copies. The sixty-six-page book, which was probably commissioned by either Menage or Mix as a souvenir, provides a wealth of information about the building in its original state and includes many photographs. A pamphlet published in 1892 called *Minneapolis and the Guaranty Loan Building* also contains a set of photographs found nowhere else. These early descriptions and photographs are particularly valuable because no full set of plans for the building is known to exist. Mix's written specifications for the building have survived and they, too, are a source of much useful information.[16]

The basic layout of the building was very straightforward, with everything organized around the light court and adjacent elevator lobbies on every floor. As built, the Guaranty Loan was divided vertically into three distinct sections. The first two floors provided commercial space. Floors three through eleven consisted of offices, many arranged as suites. There was also a law library on the tenth floor. The twelfth floor was devoted entirely to the Guaranty Loan Restaurant—the first high-rise eatery in the city and one of the few of its kind in the nation. Above the restaurant was a rooftop garden, also the first of its type in Minneapolis.

The ground floor, occupied largely by shops and small offices, was not very prepossessing. It did offer one intriguing element in the form of a glass-block floor. The same glass block, in a pattern custom made for the building, was also used on the second floor and possibly part of the third floor as well. Glass-block flooring was not a new invention in 1890 (it had been installed as early as 1879 in the rotunda of the Michigan State Capitol), but the Guaranty Loan marked its first appearance on a large scale in Minnesota. Laid in a grid of iron channels, the floor was not only beautiful but also allowed natural light to penetrate to the lowest levels of the building, including the basement. The ground floor was only partially open to the light court through a large opening cut into the ceiling. Within this opening, a grand staircase with marble treads and decorative iron railings led to the second floor after splitting into two flights near the top. Another staircase immediately below descended to the basement.

The second floor was initially occupied by three banking halls—for the Northwestern National Bank, the Security Bank of Minnesota, and the Guaranty Loan Company. Only a single early photograph hints at what these large rooms looked like. At least one of the halls was said to have frescoed walls, and other descriptions suggest that they all came with elegantly detailed tellers' windows and other deluxe furnishings typically found in banks of the time.

From the second floor, the entire light court, 56 by 90 feet, came into view. There were four hundred offices in all, arrayed around the court and its glass-floored galleries. Although some offices were occupied by professionals, including numerous lawyers, others were arranged into suites for large tenants. The city's biggest flour-milling companies, Pillsbury and Washburn-Crosby, occupied the third floor of the building, while the offices of William Washburn's Soo Line Railroad took up the entire seventh floor. Another railroad, the Minneapolis and St. Louis, had its headquarters on the eleventh floor. All offices featured large plate-glass partitions overlooking the light court and were in most cases finished with oak woodwork, maple floors, and buff-colored plaster walls. Individual offices could be rented for as little as $12.50 a month, but many tenants occupied suites and so paid a higher rate.[17]

Six-foot-wide galleries provided access to all the offices above the second

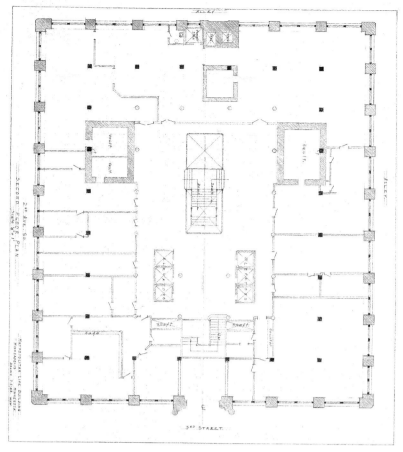

Modified second-floor plan, Metropolitan Building, circa 1960. No original set of plans for the building is known to exist. This plan, possibly based on the originals, was drawn by Walter Wheeler, a structural engineer and longtime tenant of the building.

floor. Cantilevered from the building's frame so they required no support columns, the galleries included wainscoted walls of Italian marble and ornamental cast-iron balustrades with polished brass handrails. The balustrades, which featured an intricate pattern of concentric circles and spiraling curves, were made by Crown Iron Works, a Minneapolis company founded in 1878.

All told, Crown produced more than 1,500 lineal feet of ornamental ironwork for the Guaranty Loan at a cost of $167,000, possibly the largest commission of its kind for any building in the history of Minneapolis. The pattern of the gallery

---

balustrades was largely repeated throughout the building, but a different design was employed for the railings on the grand staircase connecting the first and second floors. This design featured a long stalk with five branches at the top set at an angle into an array of circles and other curving forms.[18]

Some of the galleries around the light court incorporated one of the building's signature features: one-inch-thick translucent glass floors. Laid in 5-by-6-foot slabs, the glass was used for the galleries on floors four through nine. For the remaining galleries, Mix specified marble floors. It's likely he didn't use glass for the galleries on the upper three floors because they were close enough to the skylight to receive adequate daylighting from that source. But deeper into the building the glass gallery floors served as a means of bringing in additional light.

The light court was in every way the heart of the Guaranty Loan, a great spectacle of iron and glass that conveyed a powerful sense of modernity in sharp contrast to the building's almost antiquarian exterior. It was a bold, exciting space set beneath a 4,700-square-foot skylight described as "the largest in the Northwest." The light court must have been especially stunning at night when it was illuminated by hundreds of incandescent lights powered by three large dynamos in the basement. This direct-current electrical system was not replaced until the late 1940s, when the building was finally connected to the standard alternating current provided by the local utility.[19]

The Guaranty Loan's six passenger elevators, the most in any building of the time in Minneapolis, were arranged three to a side in lobbies on each floor at the north end of the light court. Two of the elevators protruded into the light court and their constant movement added visual excitement to the space. There was also a freight elevator located near the alley on the south side of the building.

The passenger elevators, which could go from the ground floor to the twelfth in twenty-five seconds, did not have the kind of enclosed cars that are standard today. Instead, passengers rode in cagelike, relatively lightweight iron "hatches,"

Railing detail, light court of the Metropolitan Building, 1961. More than 1,500 lineal feet of ornamental ironwork was used for gallery and staircase railings throughout the building, all of it custom made by Crown Iron Works of Minneapolis.

as they were usually called. Ornamental iron grillwork, rather than shafts, surrounded the hatches. As a result, every elevator ride was a sightseeing trip, with the workings of the building open to view. All the elevators employed operators, since automatic push-button systems did not arrive until much later. The elevators were notoriously difficult to level as they stopped at floors and so required considerable skill on the part of the uniformed operators, many of whom worked in the building for decades. They remained on the job until the building was finally vacated in 1961.

The elevators were hydraulic, powered by pistons in the basement. A series of ropes and sheaves extended the stroke of each piston so the elevators could traverse the full height of the building. Although elevators driven by electric motors became the standard for tall buildings by 1900, the Guaranty Loan's elevators

Skylight from twelfth floor, Metropolitan Building, 1961. The gallery floors here and on the two floors below were tile rather than glass, presumably because they were close enough to the skylight to receive direct daylight.

(*Above left*) Elevator cab, second floor, Metropolitan Building, 1959. The building's six open-cage hydraulic passenger elevators required operators, some of whom stayed on the job for decades. (*Above right*) Elevator screen, Metropolitan Building, 1961. Screens of filigreed ironwork, rather than shafts, protected the elevators. The screens were manufactured by the Minneapolis Wireworks Company, one of many local firms that provided fixtures and materials for the building.

were never converted. They were still in use—the last of their type in the city— when the building was demolished.

The filigreed iron screens protecting the elevators were built by the Minneapolis Wireworks Company. It was one of fifteen Minneapolis firms that contributed in one way or another to the design and construction of the building. Noting how much "home talent" worked on the project, one writer said the Guaranty Loan demonstrated "in a most credible manner the high degree of perfection that has been reached in the building line by the various trades in the city."[20]

The Guaranty Loan Restaurant that originally took up the entire twelfth floor was not only a novelty for Minneapolis but also quite possibly the only one of its kind outside of New York City. The main dining room, outfitted with antique oak furnishings and frescoed walls, overlooked Second Avenue South. It reputedly could seat up to seven hundred diners and offered views, according to one advertisement, as "high from the ground as the top of Bunker Hill Monument" in Boston. Among its amenities were linen napkins and silverware bearing the logo

(*Above left*) Advertisement for Barrett Manufacturing Company showing observation tower, circa 1890s. The rooftop garden was one of the few in the United States at the time and was particularly unusual because it was atop an office building. (*Above right*) William Allen Rogers, The Roof Garden of the Guarantee Loan Building in Minneapolis, circa 1891. Allen worked as a cartoonist and illustrator for *Harper's Weekly*, where this engraving first appeared.

of the Guaranty Loan Company. A "ladies dining room," a "gentleman's café," six private dining rooms, and a billiard room were also part of the restaurant, which stayed open until eleven o'clock at night.[21]

The restaurant was managed by Jasper Gibbs, a prominent member of the Minneapolis black community renowned for his "Southern style" cooking. Gibbs was also a civil rights activist heavily involved in, among other things, efforts to stop the lynching of blacks that occurred with cruel regularity, especially in the South. He was sufficiently well known in Minneapolis that when he married just a few months after the Guaranty Loan Restaurant opened, the wedding was duly noted in the *Tribune*. His wife, Ione, was also a community leader, and the couple eventually had five children.[22]

On summer evenings, restaurant patrons could climb a staircase to the rooftop garden, which offered chairs and tables, refreshments, regular band concerts, and a wonderful view of the city. It was also pleasantly dark, and spooning couples sometimes wandered off to the edges of the garden and carved their initials in the sandstone parapets. The lookout tower was another attraction, but it was reportedly closed at one point after a distraught young woman jumped to her death.[23]

Buildings with tall atriums have long attracted jumpers, but there do not seem to have been many suicides in the building's light court. The twenty-story light court in Chicago's Masonic Temple, for example, was said to average four suicides a year. Newspapers up until the 1950s generally made note of suicides, particularly if they occurred in public places, but in the case of the Guaranty Loan Building, few such accounts have surfaced.

$$\sim$$

The Guaranty Loan was almost surely the most expensive building ever constructed in Minneapolis when it opened in 1890. The final price tag, including the cost of the land, appears to have been about $1.8 million, an enormous expenditure at the time. The use of stone on all four sides of the building, as well as the high level of interior finishing, accounted for much of the extra expense.[24]

Louis Menage clearly wanted a monument—to himself and to the wildly successful, or so it seemed, company he had built—and he got it. The building in 1890 ruled the Minneapolis skyline, and it was hailed as proof that the young city had become the great metropolis of the Northwest. Ensconced in his tenth-floor office suite, Menage was surely proud of his achievements. His building was the toast of the city and his business appeared to be flourishing. Over the span of six years, he had risen to the top of Minneapolis, a sly and powerful king of finance seated on a wondrous throne. But his reign, shadowed by debt and chicanery, would prove short lived and in just a few years the great financier would find himself on a mule in the wilds of Guatemala, with a panier allegedly stuffed full of cash and securities, and a $5,000 award awaiting the lawman who could find him.

Downtown Minneapolis and the Northwestern Guaranty Loan Building, panoramic view from the tower of city hall, circa 1904. By this time, the Northwestern Guaranty Loan Company was defunct and its building would soon be renamed the Metropolitan.

Entrance on Second Avenue South, circa 1890. Polished granite pillars flanked an elaborately carved arch with the name "Guaranty Loan Co." worked into a banner-like frame. The globed lamp, custom made for the building, was removed in the early 1900s, as was an identical lamp in front of the Third Street entrance.

# The Northwestern Guaranty
# Loan Building, 1890–1900

H undreds of photographs of the Metropolitan Building exist, but very few
depict the building around the time of its completion in 1890. Interior
views from that era are especially rare. The images here, among the earliest ever taken of the building, are from two seldom-seen works, Ellwood
Hand's book *The Northwestern Guaranty Loan Company's Building*, published in New
York in 1890, and a booklet of unknown origin titled *Minneapolis and the Guaranty
Loan Building*, from 1892.

(*Above top*) Main entrance on Third Street, circa 1892. This entrance was similar to the one on Second Avenue South, but a bit taller. It led directly to the elevator lobby and a grand staircase to the second floor. (*Above*) Elevator lobby by main staircase on first floor, circa 1890. The first floor was largely given over to small shops and offices arranged around the building's perimeter.

Banking room of the Northwestern Guaranty Loan Company, circa 1890. This is the only known photograph of the company's business offices. Louis Menage maintained an executive suite on the tenth floor.

(*Above top*) Light court and elevators, from top of stairs on second floor, circa 1890. Three banking halls occupied this floor, which had the highest ceilings in the building. (*Above*) Main dining room on the twelfth floor, circa 1892. The Guaranty Loan Restaurant operated here for about twelve years. The man at the desk may be Jasper Gibbs, who managed the restaurant.

(*Above top*) Staircase on twelfth floor leading to rooftop garden, circa 1892. The garden was a popular spot for drinks and entertainment during the summer months, when bands regularly played in the evenings. (*Above*) Rooftop promenade and turret, circa 1892. The promenade was lined with flower beds. Part of the skylight over the inner court is visible at right. Along with its main observation tower, the building featured turrets at every corner.

# "One of the Most Colossal Swindles of the Decade"

ate in November 1890, two men met in the small New Jersey town of Bound Brook to discuss potentially explosive allegations centering on Louis Menage and the tangled affairs of the Northwestern Guaranty Loan Company. The meeting had been requested by Charles S. Bartleson, Menage's attorney, who was traveling by train from New York. The man Bartleson wanted to talk to was John H. Burke. Something of a civic gadfly in Minneapolis, Burke of late had made it his business to dig into the financial doings of Menage's company. Burke also happened to be returning from a trip east, and so after an exchange of telegrams, he and Bartleson settled on Bound Brook as a convenient place to get together.

Burke had by this time prepared a long article, which he hoped to have published in the newspapers, detailing Menage's highly questionable, and possibly even criminal, activities as president of the Guaranty Loan Company. Perhaps thinking the Minneapolis newspapers would be reluctant to publish such damaging allegations against a prominent businessman, Burke had given his article to the *St. Paul Pioneer Press*. But it languished there for weeks and in the end was never published. Even so, Burke's critique began to circulate in local financial circles and soon came to Bartleson's attention.

Exactly what was said during the meeting at Bound Brook isn't known. But in a long letter he sent a few days later to Bartleson, Burke contended that Menage was using the Guaranty Loan Company as "a sink" in which he could dump real estate acquired through "dummy" purchasers, among them clerks and janitors working for the company. The property could then be mortgaged, often for much more than it was worth, after which the loans were sold to East Coast investors, with the proceeds going into Menage's coffers. Burke went on to claim that Menage had received "some hundreds of thousands of dollars" from the company by means of these dubious maneuvers while issuing essentially worthless guarantees that the loans would be paid. It all looked like a scam to Burke, who told Bartleson that the company's books needed to be thoroughly audited and that Menage should resign at once.[1]

Bartleson disputed Burke's allegations and insisted that Menage had done nothing improper or illegal. The lawyer also let it be known that Burke's charges, if published, might well lead to a libel suit against him. Bartleson, however, did agree to discuss Burke's concerns with the Guaranty Loan Company's board of directors. In January 1891 the board reviewed the matter but did nothing to rein in Menage, who offered his resignation in response to Burke's allegations. To no one's surprise, it was not accepted, and Menage would remain president of the company until its sudden and shocking collapse.[2]

Burke, meanwhile, continued his "crusade," as the newspapers called it, against Menage and the Guaranty Loan Company. At one point Burke even accused the company of out-and-out skullduggery, claiming it hired Pinkerton agents to steal documents from his hotel room during a stay in Chicago. In early 1892 Burke took his complaints to the office of Minnesota governor William Merriam, who had served on the reception committee at the opening of the Guaranty Loan Building. It's unlikely Merriam was eager to delve into the matter, but he finally instructed State Public Examiner Moses D. Kenyon to comb through the company's books. On March 28, 1892, Kenyon issued his report, which was not remarkable for its prescience. "In general," Kenyon concluded, "the company's affairs appear to be in good condition and apparently well and carefully managed." But as Burke had divined, the company was not in good condition, and events would soon bear out his accusations.[3]

Burke's investigations did nothing to slow down Menage's frenetic pursuit of new deals in real estate, loans, and even insurance. In 1891 he concocted a scheme to issue bonds tied to policies held by Mutual Reserve Fund Life of New York, said to be the nation's fifth-largest life insurance company. The *Minneapolis*

*"One of the Most Colossal Swindles of the Decade"*

*Journal*, which could always be counted on to celebrate the city's leading business-men, said the arrangement would combine "the advantages of investment and insurance" and called it "the largest enterprise in the annals of the Northwest." The scheme, however, proved short lived because Menage, whether he knew it or not, was on a course toward disaster.[4]

～

As the 1890s began, problems buried deep in the nation's economy—depressed agricultural prices, an inadequate money supply, oceans of poorly secured debt—grew harder to ignore, and a business downturn became evident. New construction slowed, wheat prices plummeted, credit tightened. By early 1893, when much of Europe had already plunged into recession, a great unraveling began in the United States. In February of that year, the Philadelphia and Reading Railroad, thought to be a sound and well-managed company, suddenly failed under the weight of $125 million in liabilities, and the New York Stock Exchange shuddered. By early May stock prices were heading toward free fall. On May 5 the market crashed.

What followed over the next five years would be the worst depression the nation had ever experienced. Factories closed, jobs vanished amid brutal labor strife, and hard times clamped down like the lid of a coffin. Some fifteen thousand businesses, including giant railroads such as the Northern Pacific and Union Pacific, failed, as did five hundred banks. By the time the depression hit rock bottom in the mid-1890s, the nationwide unemployment rate approached 20 percent.[5]

Minneapolis was not spared. By the end of 1893, the city's superintendent of the poor, C. L. Snyder, reported that his office had received more than sixty-two hundred applications for assistance, far more than ever before, and the numbers were growing. The city helped by providing groceries and wood to needy families, but with an annual budget of $25,000, there was only so much Snyder's office could do. Wrote one historian, "Minneapolis had to pass through the fog of this depression. Her boasted thirty-eight millionaires became poor; many of her poor became beggars. . . . On some of the most promising avenues . . . rows of empty stores presented a woebegone appearance. In the newer additions empty houses and grass-grown sidewalks told the tale of inflation and hardship. Property so

As financial markets tumbled, nervous depositors staged a run on the Farmers and Mechanics Savings Bank in Minneapolis on May 19, 1893. Many banks failed during the deep depression that began that year.

depreciated in value that people began to smile whenever former prices were mentioned."[6]

Once the stock market crashed, Menage must have known that his fabulous enterprise, which had soared for years on gossamer wings of debt, was about to encounter turbulent air. During its nine years in business, the company had floated thousands of specious loans, many in the form of unsecured commercial paper, and it was also saddled with a vast amount of mortgage debt on unproductive property. In early May, as anxious creditors called in their chips, Menage worked feverishly around the clock to conjure up enough money to stave off collapse.

"Notes came due with alarming rapidity and in enormous amount," wrote Hartley Davis in the *New York Herald.* "On the 18th day of May Louis F. Menage sat all night by a telegraph wire in Minneapolis while another officer of the company" (undoubtedly Guaranty Loan's vice president Thomas Lowry) "sat in New York. They kept the wire hot with messages. Menage said that $150,000 would save

*"One of the Most Colossal Swindles of the Decade"*

Western Union Telegraph Office, Minneapolis, circa 1895. As the Guaranty Loan Company began to fail in May 1893, Louis Menage and vice president Thomas Lowry worked the telegraph lines between Minneapolis and New York in a futile effort to satisfy creditors and save the company.

them. It was forthcoming. But $150,000 was a drop in the bucket. It is doubtful if $1,500,000 would have saved them."[7]

Menage was rarely interviewed in the newspapers, preferring to work behind the scenes. It was therefore left to Lowry, who was also one of the company's largest stockholders, to deliver the bad news. He gave the first indication that the company was in grave trouble in an interview with the *Minneapolis Journal* on May 15. Lowry said that while the company had not yet suspended business, it would probably be forced to do so shortly. The company held about $3 million in commercial paper, and Lowry said, "the stringency in this money market has made it impossible for us to up or renew notes and unfortunately we cannot realize on the collateral." He said it was this financial "stringency," rather than any underlying problems with the company, that caused it to founder and claimed, falsely, "in the end the company will pay in full." Lowry added, "I have been in hourly communication today with President Menage, and here is a dispatch from him saying that with time we could pull out all right."[8]

Menage would make this claim—just a little more time and all would be well—more than once, but it was a fiction. Nonetheless, he and his allies tried their best to spin the story in the local newspapers. On May 16 the *Journal*, probably parroting what it had been told by Menage or Lowry, announced in a headline "The Affairs of the Company Not as Bad as Supposed" and "Creditors Will Lose Nothing." The *New York Times* offered an equally sunny assessment on May 28, claiming the company "would in a short time resume business, paying dollar for dollar of its indebtedness." Neither of these stories even grazed the truth. But Menage couldn't keep up the

Thomas Lowry, circa 1895. After the Northwestern Guaranty Loan Company went into bankruptcy, Lowry bought its famous building in 1895.

spin for long. As the affairs of the company unwound in bankruptcy proceedings, it became clear that Menage had been not only a fast operator of the first order but also very probably a crook.[9]

~

On May 19, 1893, the Northwestern Guaranty Loan Company went into receivership, and it marked the beginning of a long, strange, and tortuous saga that would be in the headlines for years to come. By the time it was over, there would be revelations of massive fraud, grand jury indictments, criminal trials, and a maze of civil lawsuits, all playing out while the man at the center of it—Louis Menage—was nowhere to be found. To the very end, Menage denied any wrongdoing and insisted he could fix everything if only given the chance.

The Minneapolis Trust Company was appointed as the receiver, and as its lawyers and accountants scoured the books of Menage's firm, they found much of interest. The local newspapers were slow to catch on to the unfolding scandal, however, and paid little attention to the situation. By mid-July, there were reports that Menage had "finally gone to the wall" and signed over his assets and

Guatemala City, circa 1890. Louis Menage fled to Guatemala shortly after the collapse of the Northwestern Guaranty Loan Company in 1893. A grand jury indicted him on fraud charges, but authorities were unable to locate him and bring him back to Minneapolis for trial.

liabilities to the receiver. This was true, but Menage had not done so in person, leaving the job to one of his attorneys. At about the same time the *Tribune* listed Menage as among those attending a lavish party at Lake Minnetonka. He may have been there, but it's more likely he had already left the country, perhaps as early as June 6, for points far to the south.[10]

The startling news of his departure didn't break in the local newspapers until August 13, when the *Tribune*, citing press accounts from Chicago, said Menage had fled to Chile with his office assistant, a man apparently named Edward Merritt (he was also identified as James Merritt and William Merrill in various newspaper stories). It was Merritt, according to the newspapers, who, after returning to Chicago, "casually and inadvertently" mentioned to friends that he had escorted Menage to a hideout in "the mountain fastnesses" of the South American country.[11]

Merritt may have been lying when it came to his old boss's whereabouts, which turned out to be as murky as his finances. Reports soon surfaced that Menage had actually gone to Guatemala on a ship from New Orleans. Said to be holed up in Guatemala City under the name C. A. Miller, Menage became a hunted fugitive. At some point, authorities apparently began to close in on him and he fled to Mexico.[12]

Menage's wife and sixteen-year-old daughter, whom he'd initially left behind in Minneapolis, joined him on his southern sojourn within a matter of months. Before she left, Amanda Menage sold off all the furnishings in the couple's twenty-four-room town house on Eighth Street South amid rumors she had accumulated $25,000 in cash to prepare for her journey. One newspaper also claimed Menage left Minneapolis with "a cool million" in cash and securities to tide him over, but his accountant stoutly denied that allegation, insisting Menage had taken along only a few thousand dollars in traveling money.[13]

As ever more fragrant details emerged about the extent of Menage's financial dodgery, pressure grew for criminal proceedings. A grand jury was duly convened in September 1893. The jury quickly issued subpoenas, twenty in all, to officers of the Guaranty Loan Company and members of its board. Meanwhile, the receivers had begun to figure out why the company collapsed so suddenly. Although Menage's creative use of mortgage financing drew much attention (in August, for example, the *Seattle Post-Intelligencer* offered a long account of his shady land deals in the Pacific Northwest), the Guaranty Loan's collapse stemmed mainly from its issuance of thousands of unsecured short-term notes, known as commercial paper. Essentially no more than IOUs, these notes were issued with all the care of a drunk handing out free beers at a bar, in some cases to imaginary customers.[14]

Ranging from $500 to $5,000, the notes typically came due in six months or less and carried no interest. But they could be sold at a discount to other investors and as such became a surefire money-generating scheme for the Guaranty Loan Company. The problem, as the company's receivers discovered, was that the notes were almost all fraudulent, issued to names apparently drawn at random from the Minneapolis city directories, to people who worked in the Guaranty Loan Building (among them clerks, janitors, office boys, scrubwomen, and Menage's barber), or to fictitious individuals. One clerk was listed as borrowing a total of $68,000 while a janitor who must have had expensive tastes was named on notes worth nearly $90,000. What all these "borrowers" had in common was that they had no means of paying back their loans. In most cases, they probably didn't even know they were named on the notes.[15]

Menage and his minions added one clever wrinkle to their scheme. Virtually every note was accompanied by a brief rider in the form of a testimonial as to the sterling character and financial probity of the borrower. The rider to one $2,000 note claimed, "Maker is in good shape financially to take care of his business interests and protect his paper." A rider on another note said, "Maker has by thrift and energy accumulated some property and has good reputation for promptness in business matters." The bulk of these testimonials seem to have come from Menage's fiction-writing department, since many of the supposed borrowers were never found. In one case, lawyers tried to hunt down sixty note holders but were able to identify only four as real people.

The selling of these bogus notes was entrusted chiefly to William S. Streeter, who joined the Guaranty Loan Company in 1889 and, as a vice president, quickly became Menage's right-hand man. Described as a "tall, slender man with a quiet voice," Streeter hailed from Vermont, where he once worked for a bank in the town of St. Johnsbury. It was there he made a huge number of sales, spreading the spurious notes like toxic spores through the community of sixty-five hundred people. By the time the Guaranty Loan Company collapsed, Streeter had sold $250,000 worth of notes in St. Johnsbury alone, as well as another $750,000 across Vermont. Most of the investors ended up losing every cent they had turned over to Streeter.[16]

∼

By September 1893, as the full scope of Menage's deceit became evident, the press was out for blood. In a thundering editorial, the *Tribune* declared that Menage "was the perpetrator of one of the most colossal swindles of the decade. His theft amounted to millions and his victims were numbered by the thousands. . . . His operations have done more to injure the reputation and credit of Minneapolis and Minneapolis financial enterprises than any number of failures and suspensions of the ordinary kind." But with Menage secreted somewhere in Guatemala, there was no immediate prospect of hauling him into court to face criminal charges, so authorities in Minneapolis did the next best thing by arresting Streeter.[17]

His arrest on September 19 caused what one newspaper described as a "profound sensation." Initially the only charge against him was for permitting the Guaranty Loan Company to issue a dividend without sufficient funds to pay for it. Four days later, however, a grand jury went a step further, indicting Streeter and the absent Menage on charges of stealing more than $100,000 from the company through phony loan transactions. Streeter, who had been left by his former boss to dangle in the wind, said little to the press, although he did observe, with admirable understatement, that "it would have been better had Menage remained at home."[18]

With Streeter heading toward trial, the press began to focus on the hunt for Menage. This turned out to be an unsatisfactory endeavor. Various friends, not to mention Menage's wife and daughter, seemed to have no trouble tracking him down, and at least one photograph supposedly appeared showing Menage on a mule, presumably somewhere in Guatemala or Mexico. But despite articles about Menage and his flight in newspapers from coast to coast, including the *New York Times,* the financier remained at large. In late September an exasperated editorialist for the *Tribune* wrote, "If the state cannot afford the expense of running him down, the financial institutions of Minneapolis cannot make a better investment than to co-operate with Menage's victims in raising a fund sufficient to send the best detectives to the uttermost parts of the earth, if necessary, in pursuit of him."[19]

Under public pressure, Hennepin County in early October offered a reward of $5,000 for anyone who could find Menage and bring him back to Minneapolis. Two months later, the *Tribune* reported that Hennepin County sheriff James H. Ege and a former sheriff named Winslow M. Brackett had traveled "incognito" to Washington, D.C., possibly to put pressure on the State Department to help with

## THE CITY CIRCUIT.

# ARRESTED.

William S. Streeter Taken Into Custody.

## JOHN H. BURKE COMPLAINANT.

Charged With Declaring a Fraudulent Dividend of the N. W. G. L. Company.

## HE IS HELD IN $4,000 BAIL.

The County Attorney Advised That He Intended Going Away.

## THE GRAND JURY INVESTIGATING

Twenty or Thirty Prominent Financiers Summoned to Tell What They Know.

The *Minneapolis Tribune* announced the arrest of Menage's associate, William S. Streeter, on September 20, 1893. While Menage hid in his tropical refuge, the hapless Streeter remained in Minneapolis to face criminal proceedings.

the hunt. At some point at least two newspapers in New York City, where investors had lost a great deal of money in Menage's schemes, also showed interest in joining the pursuit. So, too, did Edward Merritt, the man who had helped arrange Menage's escape. Merritt, who does not seem to have been an especially savory character, announced he would be willing to point the way to the fugitive's hideout but would first need $2,500 to loosen his tongue. He never got his money, however, and after a few months of desultory effort, the hunt for Menage petered out.[20]

On October 5, 1893, Streeter was arraigned on charges of theft and fraudulent declaration of a dividend. He pleaded not guilty. His attorney, William Lancaster, vowed to fight the charges, saying his client had committed no crime. Lancaster, in a preview of the defense's courtroom strategy, pointed to Menage as the real culprit.

Although the case against Streeter looked solid enough, it was not easy to prosecute, largely because the financial affairs of the Guaranty Loan Company were so convoluted. Hennepin County Attorney Frank Nye did not have a large office—his few assistants were mostly part-timers drawn from the local bar—and he lacked the resources needed to fully sort through the Guaranty Loan's opaque finances. Nonetheless, his office collected the evidence as best it could, and on May 28, 1894, Streeter went on trial in Hennepin County District Court.[21]

Assistant County Attorney James A. Peterson argued that Streeter was a central figure in the Guaranty Loan's fraudulent activities, peddling $3 million in worthless commercial paper on behalf of Menage, who then used the proceeds for his own speculations. "The whole business shows an enormous confidence game from the start," Peterson told the jury. More than twenty witnesses, many of them former employees of the company,

Frank M. Nye, circa 1915. As Hennepin County Attorney, Nye prosecuted William S. Streeter on charges of fraud but failed to gain a conviction after two trials in 1894.

were called on to testify as the trial dragged on for weeks. The defense argued that, contrary to the charges, Streeter had not embezzled any money from the company. His attorneys also did their utmost to paint Menage as the villainous figure behind all the company's fraudulent schemes. He had deceived Streeter, they said, just as he deceived everyone else.[22]

The case finally went to the jury on the last day of June, but no verdict was reached after a full day of deliberations. "Shut up in the big main courtroom at the old Court House, locked and bolted up, the Streeter jury hangs on, wrangling and debating," wrote the *Tribune*. "No verdict was reached last night, and at a late hour the jury was put to bed like little children in a kindergarten dormitory." Another day went by without a verdict before the jury pronounced itself hopelessly deadlocked, with eight members arguing for acquittal and four for conviction. The presiding judge then declared a mistrial and dismissed the jury.[23]

Prosecutors decided to have another go at the case, and Streeter was put on trial again in November 1894. But the second trial also ended in a hung jury, this time with the votes evenly divided between acquittal and conviction. Two days later, Nye announced that he was dismissing the indictments against Streeter.[24]

Streeter walked free just as a sensational murder case began to transfix the local press. A twenty-nine-year-old woman named Catherine Ging, known as Kittie, had been shot to death on the night of December 3 near Lake Calhoun in Minneapolis. Harry Hayward, a handsome, rakish, and quite possibly psychopathic young man about town, was soon implicated in the murder. The story became a great feast for the Minneapolis newspapers and they dined on it with unseemly gusto for months to come. With the Ging–Hayward story monopolizing the press, Streeter's case faded from memory. Menage, however, would soon make news again.[25]

∼

On February 23, 1895, as Hayward's murder trial moved into its second month, a curious letter appeared in the *Minneapolis Times*, a small daily newspaper established just six years earlier. The letter came from Menage and had purportedly been written to a "business friend" in Minneapolis. But Menage clearly intended the letter for publication, and in it he offered a series of carefully crafted justifications for the failure of the Northwestern Guaranty Loan Company and his flight to the tropics.[26]

*"One of the Most Colossal Swindles of the Decade"*

It was his optimistic spirit, he claimed, rather than any criminal wrongdoing, that led to his downfall. "As I recall the work and plans of the nine years prior to my failure I see plainly the mistakes made, the errors in judgment of an over-sanguine temperament, and regret that I did not sooner succumb to what now seems the inevitable result of carrying a heavy indebtedness, instead of increasing it, in hopes of it being finally cancelled and leaving a substantial fortune. While I can now see my mistakes and errors plainly, I fail to perceive a single step taken with the object or expectation of wrongdoing or injuring any individual or corporation." He added that "had the financial sky remained bright a short time longer, I have every reason to believe that the enterprises in which I was engaged would have been successfully carried out."

Menage went on at length to review his business career, including the costly lawsuit brought against him by William King in the 1880s. He also offered an almost risible explanation for his sudden move to Guatemala. The strain of the company's bankruptcy and "the ignominy attached to defeat and failure," he wrote, left him "so completely prostrated mentally and physically" that doctors told him he must "secure relief" at once. "I felt that remaining at home meant either death or a mental asylum, and when going away seemed to promise recovery of health by entire change, in justice to my family, my creditors, and myself the trip was undertaken."

It's doubtful anyone really believed Menage was traveling for his health, as opposed to trying to avoid prosecution. Even so, he went on with breathtaking chutzpah to state that he would be happy to return to Minneapolis "to assist in the settling of the estates, if allowed a salary to support my family, and to take such efforts as may be [in] my power to pay claims both against me and the company and prevent further loss to the stockholders." In exchange for this generous offer, all Menage asked was that the criminal charges against him be dropped, not only because he was innocent but also because a trial would "involve so much time" that he wouldn't be able to undertake the noble work of helping out his creditors. He added, with characteristic optimism, "in five years I should hope to see all claims very much reduced if not paid in full."

It was an offer both the Minneapolis Trust Company, which was handling the bankruptcy, and Hennepin County Attorney Frank Nye were fully able to resist. An official with the trust company scoffed at the offer, saying, "It is a late day now to attempt to save anything. The entanglements of the estate have gone so

far that they are past unraveling." Nye's
response was equally succinct. "The laws
of the state permit no bargaining with
men under indictment," he said. "If Menage came back it would be my duty to
prosecute him . . . as soon as practicable."

So Menage stayed on in Guatemala,
where, according to one account, he had
taken up a new career as a coffee broker.
Although Menage was not said to be acquiring great wealth in this endeavor, he
apparently had sufficient money to bribe
Guatemalan officials if need be to avoid
returning to the United States. "You
could not bring him back forcefully,"
said a man who had talked with him. "It
would take $20,000 in cold cash to do it,
for you would have to pay up all the native
officials, and Menage has a good hold on
them now."[27]

Menage—Can I come back?
Nye—Cert! come on.

Cartoon showing Louis Menage in
Honduras and Hennepin County Attorney Frank Nye beckoning him back to
Minnesota, *Minneapolis Times*, February
23, 1895. It's unlikely Menage was ever
in Honduras, but there was much uncertainty over his whereabouts after he
fled Minneapolis.

~

The building that had been Menage's monument also held some secrets. Shortly
after the Guaranty Loan Company plunged into bankruptcy, its receivers made a
startling discovery. They had assumed the building was a prime asset that could
be sold to help pay off creditors. But they soon learned that the company no longer owned the building or had so much as a cent of equity in it. Instead, the building had been sold in 1891 to a new corporation created by Menage, who somehow
neglected to file any record of the transaction until the day before the Guaranty
Loan Company went bankrupt.[28]

Menage may have spun off the building to a new corporate entity as part of a
plan to sell it. There are indications that a buyer was in the wings and willing to pay
top dollar for the building, but as the economy began to sink the deal fell through.
Menage and many of his associates, including Thomas Lowry, were presumably

among the principals of the Guaranty Loan Building Company, as the new corporation was called. In 1895, as the Guaranty Loan Company's complex bankruptcy proceedings began to wind down, Lowry purchased the building, which carried a $600,000 mortgage. It's not known how much he paid for it or what the terms were, but as a former vice president of the Guaranty Loan Company, he was as familiar with the building as anyone, and he would own it for the next ten years.[29]

Not long after Lowry purchased the building, the *Chicago Tribune* reported that Menage had been murdered in Honduras. Like so many of the wisps of news that floated around the discredited financier, the report turned out to be false. Menage remained very much alive, although his whereabouts were as uncertain as ever. Eventually, however, he and his family migrated to Mexico, where they lived for a time in Mexico City and later in Cuernavaca, about fifty miles to the south. True to form, he dealt in real estate in Cuernavaca, a city known for its beautiful setting and mild climate.[30]

But Menage averred that he always wanted to return to Minneapolis, and in 1899 he finally did so. "Menage Is Back" proclaimed a story in the *Minneapolis Tribune* on June 29. The story included a long interview with Menage, who reiterated his innocence, claimed yet again that only poor health had caused him to leave Minneapolis, and continued to maintain that he hoped one day "to pay every dollar that I owe." Accompanied by his attorney, Charles S. Bartleson, Menage was then arraigned on a total of three grand jury indictments, handed down in 1893 and 1894, which accused him of stealing close to $1 million from the Guaranty Loan Company. Menage pled not guilty on all counts and was released on a $10,000 bond.[31]

Menage probably came back to Minneapolis when he did because he thought that after a six-year absence, there was little chance the criminal case against him could be successfully prosecuted, especially in light of what had happened in Streeter's two trials. Menage was right. In December 1899 Hennepin County Attorney Louis Reed, staring at the joyless prospect of a long courtroom slog through the financial morasses of the Guaranty Loan Company, moved to dismiss all charges. Reed noted that many potential witnesses were no longer available and that the two hundred or so exhibits offered as evidence in Streeter's trials could not be found, thereby making any prosecution of Menage extremely difficult. Hennepin County District judge Charles Pond agreed, saying he had "grave doubts that a prima facie case could be made out against Menage."[32]

Free at last from the threat of criminal prosecution, Menage still had to contend with civil lawsuits stemming from his company's demise, and it appears he remained in Minneapolis for some time. In the end, however, few if any of his many creditors were made whole, and by the early 1900s the meteor that had been the Northwestern Guaranty Loan Company gave out its last sporadic flashes in the county courts. Menage, meanwhile, moved on, ultimately settling in New Jersey.

But the building that had been his one great creation stood as solid as ever against the Minneapolis skyline. Lowry owned the building until 1905, when he

sold it to the Metropolitan Life Insurance Company of New York. Thereafter, through a succession of owners that included New York governor and one-time presidential candidate Al Smith, the building was known as the Metropolitan Life or simply the Metropolitan, and it, too, would encounter hard times as downtown Minneapolis remade itself in the twentieth century.[33]

---

Metropolitan Building on the Minneapolis skyline, circa 1906. The building acquired its new name after Thomas Lowry sold it to the Metropolitan Life Insurance Company of New York in 1905.

# "The Lower Loop Is Sunk"

When the Guaranty Loan Building became the Metropolitan Life in 1905, the Gateway area could no longer be fairly described as the commercial heart of downtown Minneapolis. Downtown's largest department stores—Donaldson's, Powers, and Dayton's—had already established themselves to the south along Nicollet Avenue. New office buildings were also rising nearby. One of them, the sixteen-story Soo Line–First National Bank Building at Fifth Street and Marquette Avenue, eclipsed the Metropolitan as the city's tallest skyscraper in 1914. Other big changes were also occurring. Between 1903 and 1912, a wave of large new hotels (the Andrews, Curtis, Dyckman, Leamington, and Radisson, among others) pushed as far south as Tenth Street. City government left the Gateway as well, abandoning the old city hall on Bridge Square in favor of the gigantic new Municipal Building.

The Gateway nonetheless remained vibrant, if more than a little shabby in places. As many as 250,000 people still passed through the district every year, among them thousands of seasonal workers drawn to its hiring halls and growing collection of flophouses. Within eyeshot of Gateway Park, a dozen employment agencies hired men year-round to cut timber, harvest crops, lay railroad

Soo Line–First National Bank Building, Fifth Street and Marquette Avenue, 1915. The sixteen-story skyscraper, which opened in 1914, eclipsed the Metropolitan as the city's tallest building.

Edward Shelland Saloon, 116 Hennepin Avenue, circa 1905. The Gateway area was home to a hundred or more saloons by 1900. Few were elegant.

tracks, and provide labor of all kinds. The district also offered one commodity—alcohol—that was not available elsewhere downtown, or in most other parts of Minneapolis, because of "liquor patrol limits" put in place by the city in the 1880s. Under the limits, saloons serving hard liquor were restricted to the Gateway area, parts of Northeast Minneapolis, and the Cedar–Riverside neighborhood. Elsewhere in the city, drinking establishments could serve nothing stronger than beer with a maximum alcohol content of 3.2 percent.[1]

The Gateway's concentration of saloons (there were already ninety-three by 1888 and even more by 1900) was a boon to drinkers but also gave much of the district an unsavory reputation for rowdiness and disarray. Even so, it was not yet the down-and-out skid row that would make it ripe for urban renewal in the 1950s. Good-sized department and clothing stores still flourished, as did many first-class hotels such as the Vendome and Rogers on Fourth Street. Some of downtown's largest office buildings, led by the Metropolitan, also remained in the district. Another important presence was Janney, Semple, Hill and Company, a wholesale hardware firm that maintained a warehouse complex at First Street and Marquette Avenue.[2]

Although hardly in critical condition, the Gateway by the early 1900s was clearly in need of rejuvenation, especially in its historic core around Bridge Square, where buildings that in some cases dated back to the 1860s formed a decaying, densely packed environment. City leaders, meanwhile, were already thinking about ways to revitalize the district and would continue to do so over the next fifty years as the Gateway became the target of numerous improvement plans. Some were enormously ambitious, others quite modest, and only a few were carried out. But they did change the district in significant ways well before the vast cleansing of the Gateway Center urban renewal project began. The Metropolitan Building was never seriously endangered by the revitalization efforts that occurred before the 1950s, but the city's persistent dream of remaking the Gateway ultimately led to its destruction.

$\sim$

On December 2, 1906, the *Minneapolis Journal* published a lengthy story devoted to what it described as "a striking and comprehensive plan for laying out Minneapolis on new lines of use and beauty." Illustrated by a map that took up almost a full page of the newspaper, the plan was the work of a team of four architects led by John Jager, who had trained in Vienna before immigrating to Minneapolis in 1902. The plan was nothing if not bold. It called for refashioning much of downtown by means of new public squares, diagonal streets, riverside boulevards, and bridges. It also envisioned a new Union Station and plaza at Second Street and Second Avenue South, an exposition building and public baths on Nicollet Island, and a five-block-long public concourse between Third and Fourth Streets and Fifth and Tenth Avenues South. Adjacent to the concourse, north of the Municipal Building, Jager proposed a great square, around which three additional public buildings could be located, thereby creating a true civic center.[3]

The *Journal* acknowledged that Jager's plan, which would have cost a fortune to carry out, "may seem at first blush utopian and impractical." It was all of that, and it never advanced much beyond its beautiful map. Yet the plan's call for a civic center and concourse along Third and Fourth Streets proved to be prophetic, and schemes advancing similar ideas would reappear periodically all the way through the 1950s.

Two years after Jager's plan appeared, a far more limited scheme for improving the Gateway emerged from an unlikely source: the Minneapolis Park Board.

**THE SUNDAY JOURNAL.**

*Editorial Section* **Part II.**

MINNEAPOLIS, MINNESOTA, SUNDAY MORNING, DECEMBER 2, 1906.

**STRIKING AND COMPREHENSIVE PLAN FOR LAYING OUT
MINNEAPOLIS ON NEW LINES OF USE AND BEAUTY**

THE CENTRAL DISTRICT OF MINNEAPOLIS AS LAID OUT IN THE JAGER-S TRAUS-EDWINS-HALDEN PLAN.

Architect John Jager's plan for Minneapolis, 1906. The plan called for the creation of a new public concourse in the heart of the Gateway district. The plan, which would have required vast expenditures, was never carried out.

Jesse Northrup, the board's president, floated the idea of creating a new park in the heart of the district just south of Bridge Square. The idea quickly gained support. Although Bridge Square already functioned as a public space of sorts, it was little more than a wide spot at the intersection of Hennepin and Nicollet Avenues, with no amenities to recommend it. Plans were already in the works for an imposing new railroad station, the Great Northern, at the foot of Hennepin, and a new park, Northrup believed, would serve as a welcoming "gateway" to travelers while also providing much needed green space downtown.

West side of Nicollet Avenue from Second Street, toward Washington Avenue, 1913. The buildings here were some of the oldest in Minneapolis. All of them were razed to make way for Gateway Park.

In December 1908, while the Park Board was still weighing Northrup's idea, Minneapolis-based *Western Architect* magazine published three proposals from local architects showing what the new Gateway Park, as it was called, might look like. The site being considered for the park consisted of a pair of wedge-shaped blocks between Nicollet and Hennepin Avenues, and Washington Avenue and First Street South. Neither block was among the jewels of the city. The smaller of the two, between Second and First Streets, was occupied by only one building—the old city hall, an ungainly stone hulk that had been largely vacated after the completion of the new Municipal Building. The adjacent block, between Second Street and Washington Avenue, was larger and contained a tight jumble of aging stone and brick buildings. Saloons—an estimated twenty-seven in all—occupied more than a few of these buildings, and one of the park plan's selling points, which would be echoed fifty years later in the Gateway Center project, was that it promised to improve a badly blighted portion of the city.[4]

In presenting the park proposals, *Western Architect* took the usual rhetoric of renewal a step further, contemptuously describing the two blocks as "an unsightly pile of rubbish." The magazine added, "No more argument should be needed than in removing a dump heap from the front yard of a private residence." And in what might be called the sanitary argument, the magazine went on to observe that "the greatest force toward civic advancement is cleanliness. The downtown district needs a clean shirt, and needs it worse than any city of its size and possibilities that we know of."

In 1909, with the full support of recently appointed parks superintendent Theodore Wirth, the Park Board agreed to purchase the two blocks, level them, and create Gateway Park. It would be the first publicly financed urban renewal project in the city's history, and not everyone thought it was a good idea. Acquiring the two blocks and tearing down all of the buildings carried a hefty price tag of $643,000, and critics believed it was far too much to spend for barely more than an acre of land. There was another big expense as well because the Park Board decided to build a large pavilion in the park, at a cost exceeding $100,000. Designed by Minneapolis architect Edwin Hewitt, who had produced one of the proposals for *Western Architect,* the pavilion was a lovely Beaux-Arts structure with curving colonnades on either side of a domed centerpiece.[5]

The old city hall was demolished in 1912 after a fire, but the other block, occupied by more than fifteen buildings, was not cleared until late in 1913, when construction of the park's pavilion began. The pavilion was finished a year later. Carved over its entrance were the words "More than her gates, the city opens her heart to you." Perhaps more important, the city opened a "comfort station" in the pavilion. The new public bathrooms proved to be extremely popular, serving an astounding nine thousand users a day at their peak.

When he first proposed the park, Northrup told the *Minneapolis Tribune* he was "fully persuaded" it would attract "busy, respectable people" as opposed to "loafers" and "tramps." But the Gateway's large population of retirees and seasonally unemployed men was inevitably drawn to the park, especially during the summer months, and it turned into exactly the kind of hangout Northrup denied it would become. The park also proved costly to operate, consuming far more in annual maintenance funds than its size seemed to justify.[6]

As plans were being laid for Gateway Park in 1909, a group of Minneapolis businessmen with far larger aspirations for the neighborhood and the rest of the city began to hold regular meetings. Joined by a token representative from labor, the businessmen formed what came to be known as the Civic Commission, and then hired Chicago architects Daniel Burnham and Edward Bennett to prepare a plan with the potential to reshape the entire city. Burnham was a nationally recognized figure, having vaulted to prominence as director of works for the World's Columbian Exposition in Chicago in 1893. Renowned for its gleaming "White City" of plaster-clad buildings, the fair touched off a new era of classically inspired architecture in the United States. It also led to the rise of the so-called City Beautiful movement, which sought to bring a measure of Parisian-style grandeur and order to American cities. Just before being hired by the Minneapolis commission, Burnham and Bennett had produced their *Plan of Chicago*, one of the movement's defining documents.[7]

Bennett was in charge of the Minneapolis project. The result of his work, completed in 1912 but not published until 1917, was the *Plan of Minneapolis*, a gorgeously impractical dream that conjured up a city of monumental boulevards and magnificent vistas, ornate Beaux-Arts public buildings, vast squares, and riverfront promenades. Along with its grandiose plans, the 228-page document managed to include much useful information. Among other things, it confirmed, by examining the destinations of streetcar riders, that the city's commercial core had moved away from the Gateway. With that in mind, the plan called for a new civic center complex to be located near Eighth Street and Portland Avenue, well south of the site Jager had favored. For the Gateway, the plan envisioned three major interventions—a new plaza at the foot of Hennepin Avenue in front of the soon-to-be completed Great Northern Station, a diagonal extension of Park Avenue linking the plaza to the Municipal Building, and the construction of parks and boulevards along the riverfront.[8]

While the *Plan of Minneapolis* was being touted, the Bridge Square area received a boost with the opening of the new Great Northern Station in 1914. The station was built directly across Hennepin Avenue from the cramped old Union Depot that had served rail passengers since 1885. A solid example of the Beaux-Arts style popular at the turn of the century, the station would remain a powerful architectural presence at Bridge Square until its demolition in 1978.

A year after the station opened, another big project, a new U.S. Post Office,

Gateway Park and Pavilion, circa 1916. The park, dedicated in 1915, was the first publicly financed urban renewal project in the city's history. The elegant pavilion was razed in 1953 and the park itself disappeared in another round of urban renewal in the 1960s.

transformed an entire block in the Lower Loop along Washington Avenue between Second and Third Avenues South. More than twenty buildings were razed to make way for the post office. Meanwhile, its 1889 predecessor, next to the Metropolitan Building, continued to be used as a federal courts and office building. The new post office (now a federal office building) quickly proved to be inadequate, and it was replaced just nineteen years later by a far larger facility a few blocks away.[9]

Both the Great Northern Station and the post office were incorporated into the *Plan of Minneapolis*, which for the most part proved to be a paper dream with little practical effect. But along with Jager's work, it introduced the idea of large-scale urban planning to Minneapolis. For the next forty years, however, only a lim-

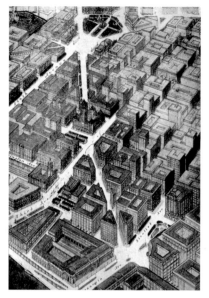

Proposed new streets and boulevards in the Gateway area, *Plan of Minneapolis*, 1917. Inspired by the so-called City Beautiful movement, the plan would have remade much of downtown Minneapolis.

ited amount of redevelopment took place in the Gateway. Elsewhere downtown the story was different. The 1920s in particular saw a huge series of changes as skyscrapers rose to unprecedented heights, dozens of old mansions fell to the wrecker, and new owners took control of the Metropolitan Building.

Like the 1880s, the 1920s were a boom time in downtown Minneapolis. The city was still growing at a sprightly pace—between 1900 and 1930 its population more than doubled from 203,000 to 464,000—and downtown development reflected this trend. Although scores of new buildings were constructed during the first two decades of the century and many others were razed, the rate of growth accelerated in the 1920s as downtown continued to expand to the west and south of the Gateway.

The Victorian-era mansions that still occupied many blocks along and south of Seventh Street were especially vulnerable to redevelopment. "Most of them," the *Minneapolis Journal* noted in 1921, "are shabby, run down and decrepit, awaiting

William W. Harrison House, Eighth Street and Second Avenue South, awaiting demolition, 1921. Built in about 1870, the Harrison House was one of many mansions razed in the 1920s as commercial expansion reshaped downtown Minneapolis.

the inevitable day when the wreckers will pull them down for new business blocks." In many cases, they did not have to wait long. Three of the city's most prominent mansions from the 1870s—the William Judd House at Fifth Street and Portland Avenue, the Alonzo Rand House at Seventh and Portland, and the Curtis Pettit House at Tenth Street and Second Avenue South—came down between 1923 and 1926. All told, more than fifty downtown mansions and scores of smaller homes were demolished by the end of the decade.[10]

Small commercial blocks, industrial buildings, and apartment houses filled in many of the lots where the mansions had been cleared away. Closer to the commercial core, in the blocks around the so-called 100 percent corner of Seventh Street and Nicollet Avenue, new office towers, stores, theaters, and institutional buildings rose from the ruins of the past. Just as the decade of the 1880s had culminated with a burst of new construction in 1888 and 1889, the 1920s came to an end on a high note with the completion of such landmarks as the Minnesota

Nicollet Hotel with Gateway Park in foreground, 1924. The new hotel, later known as the Pick-Nicollet, was built with the help of a campaign that raised $3 million from the public.

——————————

(later Radio City) Theater (1928), the Rand Tower and the Foshay Tower (both 1929), and the Northwestern National Bank Building (1930).[11]

The Gateway, still dominated by the hulking presence of the Metropolitan Building, attracted much less in the way of new construction, although two new hotels—the Ritz (later Minnesota) and the Nicollet, both completed in 1924—gave hope that the district might be able to shed its growing reputation as the city's skid row. The Ritz, at Washington and Second Avenues South, was relatively small, with about 200 rooms. The Nicollet was a much bigger project. The twelve-story, 637-room hotel occupied the site of the historic Nicollet House on Washington Avenue between Hennepin and Nicollet. Plans to replace the Nicollet House, parts of which dated to 1858, had surfaced as early as 1912. But it was only after structural and safety issues forced the aging hotel to close in 1923 that serious work began on a successor. With the help of the city, a financial drive raised $3 million through the public sale of stocks and bonds to build the new Nicollet.[12]

The hotel enjoyed substantial patronage in the 1920s, and its presence just a few blocks from the Metropolitan Building helped shore up the immediate neighborhood, which, like most of the Gateway, showed increasing signs of decay. Later renamed the Pick-Nicollet, the hotel, because of its size and relatively good condition, escaped demolition during the Gateway Center project and remained in business until 1973.[13]

Although the two new hotels helped give a respectable air to parts of the Gateway, much of it continued its rough life as the city's honky-tonk quarter, where all the usual vices

Prohibition raid on Washington Avenue, circa 1925. The Gateway's bars turned to serving soft drinks during Prohibition, but alcohol was not difficult to find in many establishments.

flourished. Prohibition in theory had shut down the district's numerous saloons, but many were quickly recast as "soft drink" bars. Coca-Cola may indeed have been available in some of these establishments, but others offered stronger libations and also became thinly disguised fronts for gambling and prostitution. A Hennepin County grand jury convened in 1922 to investigate the mischief was allegedly shocked to discover more than thirty brothels operating within an area of just four square blocks near First Street and Marquette Avenue. Sin, it seemed, remained the one indestructible enterprise in the Gateway.[14]

Despite the Gateway's sagging reputation, the Metropolitan Building, located a block south of Washington Avenue and its beckoning lineup of bars and cheap hotels, continued to be a decent, if no longer prime, business address through the 1920s. The building's tenant mix by 1922 was highly varied, led by a large group of railroad freight agents. But the Metropolitan did begin to lose major tenants as newer, better-equipped downtown office buildings siphoned off some of its old clientele. The banks that had once occupied grand halls on the second floor moved elsewhere, as did the corporate offices of the Washburn-Crosby Company (which in 1928 became General Mills). Also gone was the twelfth-floor Guaranty Loan Restaurant, where Jasper Gibbs had practiced his "Southern style" cooking. It closed around 1902, although the roof garden above remained in operation for several more years.[15]

~

As Minneapolis took its first steps toward improving the Gateway, Louis Menage began to build a new life for himself and his family. After the indictments against him were dismissed in 1899, he remained in Minneapolis for a year or two. He declared personal bankruptcy but was still embroiled in lawsuits brought by creditors trying to reclaim something from the debacle of 1893. Despite his legal and financial troubles, Menage kept making real estate deals, and in September 1900 he journeyed to Galveston, Texas, to check on some property.

He was there on September 8 when a powerful hurricane, the most lethal natural disaster in American history, roared into the island city with 145-mile-an-hour winds and a 15-foot-high storm surge. By the time it was over, an estimated 6,000 to 8,000 people, and possibly as many as 12,000, were dead. Menage somehow managed to escape without injury, a fate not everyone felt was in accord with the principles of divine justice. Recalling the devastation caused by the Guaranty Loan Company's failure, the *St. Paul Daily Globe* wrote, "When this news [of Menage's survival] reaches the quiet homes of penniless widows in Vermont and New Hampshire, who saw their fortunes wiped out in that wreck of bogus notes and other fraudulent devices, it will not be surprising if, in previously devout homes, there spread to some extent a heretical respect for the popular but irreverent saying that 'the devil takes care of his own.' "[16]

In 1902 Menage relocated to Chicago, where he became president of a speculative venture called the Mount Shasta Gold Mining Company. The *Minneapolis Journal* reported that Menage, who by this time had emerged from bankruptcy, was living comfortably with his family in a "fashionable apartment building." The newspaper added, "Friends who have seen him recently declare that he has resumed his old air of urbanity and that he is on the highway to success. They say, too, that he is little changed from the Menage of old, except that his beard is now

At least six thousand people and possibly many more died in the hurricane that devastated Galveston, Texas, on September 8, 1900. Louis Menage was in Galveston on business that day but managed to ride out the storm without injury.

snow white. . . . There seems to be every prospect that he will again be a rich man within a few years."[17]

Menage's hopes of making a new fortune in gold never panned out, and before long he was on the move again, this time to New Brunswick, New Jersey, about forty miles south of New York City. There, he went back to dealing in real estate, with an office at 220 Broadway in Manhattan. It does not appear, however, that he ever again became involved in anything on the grand scale of the Guaranty Loan Company.

Menage remained in New Jersey until his death, of a heart attack, on March 15, 1924, at age seventy-one. In the quotidian world of the press, Menage was ancient news, but his passing did produce a decent-sized obituary in the *Minneapolis Journal*. The obituary revisited his financial skullduggery and Guatemalan adventures in some detail yet also identified him, with little regard for all the pain he had caused, as "the most tragic figure in connection with the financial upheavals of 1893." The *Tribune* offered a far briefer obituary, much of which was cribbed from the *Journal*'s story. A newspaper in New Jersey also noted Menage's death, but made no mention of his checkered career in Minneapolis.[18]

Just two weeks after Menage's death, a syndicate of New York investors purchased the Metropolitan Life Building, as it was then known, for $1.3 million, considerably less than what it had cost to build thirty-four years earlier. One of the investors, L. N. Rosenbaum, told the *Minneapolis Tribune* that the new owners planned to undertake $50,000 to $100,000 worth of improvements, including new elevators, remodeling of the two lower floors and cleaning of the soot-stained exterior. Few of these planned improvements, however, were ever carried out.[19]

In 1929 the building changed hands again, for an undisclosed price. The new owner was a New York real estate firm headed by Al Smith. A former governor of New York, Smith had been the Democratic Party's presidential candidate in 1928. After losing to Herbert Hoover, Smith took up a career in real estate and later led the corporation that built and managed New York's Empire State Building, which became the world's tallest skyscraper when it was completed in 1931.[20]

By the time Smith's company bought the Metropolitan Building, there were many signs of trouble in the American economy. Commodity prices were depressed, banks were failing at an alarming rate (some 235 in Minnesota alone, mostly in rural areas, went under between 1920 and 1926), and debt was at record levels. Still, no was one prepared for what was to come.

The stock market crash in October 1929 brought the giddy, gin-soaked days of the Jazz Age to an abrupt end, and the Great Depression soon lodged itself in American life like a bone-deep wound that seemed as though it might never heal. In Minneapolis the depression struck the Gateway and its denizens especially hard. By the early 1930s squatter shacks cobbled together from waste wood formed an impromptu community along the riverfront just north of downtown, while the Gateway's missions struggled to feed and shelter an army of unemployed men. Other unemployed men congregated in Gateway Park, especially during the summer months.[21]

The depression was as hard on buildings as it was on people. Owners of old mansions and apartment buildings struggled to keep up with taxes, and they sometimes opted for demolition as a last resort. At least three dozen historic mansions, apartments, and row houses in the downtown area alone were razed during the 1930s. At the same time, a number of large downtown office buildings became vacant, among them E. Townsend Mix's picturesque old Globe Building

Unemployed men lounging in Gateway Park, 1937. Nearby missions provided food and shelter, but their resources were strained to the limit as the Great Depression wore on.

(*Above*) Marlborough Hotel fire, Fifteenth Street and Third Avenue South, January 3, 1940. Nineteen people died when fire raced through the fifty-one-year-old row house, also known as the Marlborough Flats. As many as 120 people may have been living in the building at the time. (*Opposite*) Workers removing the upper floors of the Oneida Building, Fourth Street and Marquette Avenue, 1942. The seven-story Oneida was cut down to two stories, possibly to reduce its tax load. The Metropolitan Building is in the background.

on Fourth Street. Some owners even took the drastic step of lopping floors off their buildings as a way to reduce tax bills. The Oneida Building, constructed in 1888 at Fourth Street and Marquette Avenue, closed for a time during the early 1930s and was later cut down from seven stories to just two. A number of smaller buildings around the city were downsized in similar fashion.[22]

As the Great Depression dragged on, the old apartment buildings in and around downtown became packed with families or groups of roommates doubling up to afford the rent. The three-story Marlborough Hotel at Fifteenth Street and Third Avenue South was typical in this regard. Built in 1889 as a row house, it was home by 1940 to perhaps 120 residents occupying eighteen apartments.

"Barmaid District" before being cleared for Pioneer Square, 1932. Seedy bars and prostitution once flourished on this block, which was bounded by First and Second Streets and Marquette and Second Avenues South.

On January 3 of that year, flames raced through the building with disastrous results. Nineteen people died and many others were injured in what remains the deadliest fire in the city's history.[23]

Private construction in Minneapolis and elsewhere around the nation all but stopped during the depths of the depression. But after Franklin D. Roosevelt won the presidency in 1932, his administration moved to revive the economy through a massive program of public works. One such project, completed in 1938 under the auspices of the federal Public Works Administration, was Minnesota's first public housing project—Sumner Field in North Minneapolis. Thirty acres of slum housing were cleared away for Sumner Field, which was a preview of much larger urban renewal projects to come in the 1950s.[24]

The Gateway also became the scene of a big federal project in the 1930s when the government decided to construct a new U.S. Post Office—the third built in the area within a span of less than fifty years. Completed in 1934, the art deco–style building extended for more than a block along the north side of First Street between Marquette and Second Avenue South. The project wasn't limited to the new building, however. The federal government also wanted a block of decrepit buildings in front of the Post Office to be cleared away.

Bounded by First and Second Streets and Marquette and Second Avenue South, the block was regarded as a municipal disgrace, not only because of its rundown buildings. By the late 1920s, it had become home to floating prostitution rings that cropped up after the city closed down most of the brothels that had once operated on First Street and later

Dedication of sculpture in Pioneer Square, with new U.S. Post Office in background, November 11, 1936. The park is gone, replaced by an apartment building, and artist John Karl Daniels's granite sculpture is now in northeast Minneapolis.

along Eleventh Avenue South. The rings conducted their business out of several seedy saloons on the block, which was euphemistically described in the press as the "Barmaid District."[25]

The federal government didn't want its new post office to overlook such disreputable goings-on, and so the city and the Minneapolis Park Board agreed to purchase the entire block for just under $500,000 and wipe it clean in order to create a new park called Pioneer Square. By the end of 1932 all the block's more than twenty old buildings had been swept away. The park itself wasn't dedicated until 1936, when a large granite sculpture by John Karl Daniels called *Pioneers* was installed as its centerpiece.

Like nearby Gateway Park, Pioneer Square did little to change the ambience of the Gateway. Instead, it became just another spot for lounging and drinking, and after the annual spring snowmelt, crews sometimes removed enough wine and whiskey bottles from the park to fill seventy bushel baskets. The park continued to host its well-fortified clientele until the Gateway Center project transformed the area in the 1960s. By that time the city saw no use for the park and it was removed. An apartment tower was later built on the block, some years after the *Pioneers* sculpture had been relocated to a new setting in Northeast Minneapolis.[26]

The post office was by far the largest construction project in the Gateway during the 1930s, but other plans soon began circulating to remake the district on a grand scale. In 1940, for example, Minneapolis City councilman Edwin A. Hendricks offered a scheme he dubbed "Washington Boulevard." The idea was to nearly double Washington Avenue's width to 178 feet, run streetcar tracks down the middle, and then demolish all the old buildings on either side of the new boulevard between Hennepin Avenue and the Mississippi River. Hendricks claimed his plan would "clear away a 15-block row of unsightly buildings and force construction of modern buildings to replace them."[27]

Hendricks's plan generated no support, but a consensus was nonetheless developing among city leaders that the Gateway, which by this time was also known as the Lower Loop, had to be fixed, and not in piecemeal fashion. Lewis C. Mills, writing in the *Minneapolis Star Journal*, put it this way in 1940: "In plain language, the lower loop is sunk; it has reached an advanced state of decay and, allowed to follow its natural course, another 10 years merely will find it approaching complete disintegration. . . . With 10 or a dozen exceptions, every building below Fourth Street may be a parking lot 10 years from now." Mills didn't have the timing quite right but his apocalyptic projections were not far off the mark. Once the nation fought its way through World War II, the Gateway and much of downtown Minneapolis would be ripe for renewal on an unprecedented scale.[28]

Two years after Mills sounded the death knell for the Gateway, the Metropolitan Building was sold for a fifth time. The purchaser was a previous owner, the Metropolitan Life Insurance Company. Yet another set of owners—the last—took over in 1946. By then, the building was already being eyed as a target for demolition, but it would be fifteen years before the wrecking crews arrived.

# "How Sick Is This Heart of Minneapolis?"

When World War II ended in 1945, veterans returned home to find a severe housing shortage in Minnesota and throughout the United States. The roots of the shortage went back to a dramatic decline in new home construction during the early years of the Great Depression. Then, with home construction already lagging, the war made matters worse because of strict limits on new building imposed by the federal government. The city of Minneapolis, for example, issued just three residential building permits for all of 1943.[1]

The postwar housing crunch became the impetus for two important pieces of legislation that paved the way for large-scale, publicly financed urban renewal in Minneapolis and other American cities. The process began at the state level, when the Minnesota legislature in 1947 passed the Municipal Housing and Redevelopment Act, which authorized Minneapolis, St. Paul, and other cities to undertake slum clearance and urban renewal. Shortly after the law was passed, the Minneapolis City Council created the city's first Housing and Redevelopment Authority. The Minneapolis HRA, which held its initial meeting in November 1947, would become the prime mover behind the Gateway Center project and its immense program of clearance. The agency's offices were located for many years on the twelfth floor of the Metropolitan Building, which it would later work with unwavering diligence to destroy.[2]

Minnesota's act went into effect as Congress debated new housing legislation on a much larger scale. These efforts came to fruition in the Housing Act of

Offices of the Minneapolis Housing and Redevelopment Authority, room 1214, Metropolitan Building, 1959. The agency by this time had already decided to demolish the building.

1949. Among its many provisions was the creation of a new federal urban renewal program designed to help cities like Minneapolis clear out "blighted areas" and build new public housing. In its initial form, the act focused on slum clearance in residential districts. It was later amended, however, to make other types of areas eligible for federal urban renewal aid, a change that opened the way for the Gateway Center project.

The new legislation came along as Minneapolis civic leaders continued to explore plans for remaking the Gateway area, which by then was commonly referred to in city documents and newspaper stories as the Lower Loop. In 1945 a group called the Civic Center Development Association unveiled a grand scheme that was largely the work of architect Robert Cerny, who would play a key role in

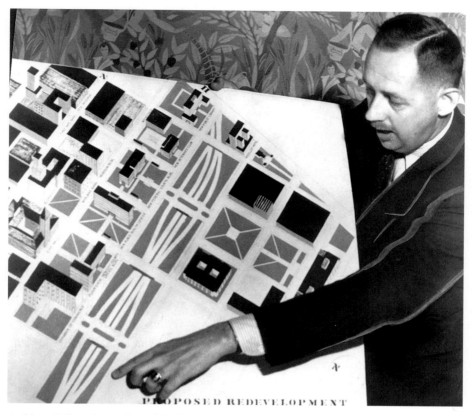

Architect Robert Cerny shows his plan for remaking the Gateway area, circa 1945. Cerny's plan called for several new civic buildings, some of which were built years later.

the redevelopment of the Gateway for years to come. The group had formed in response to a presentation by Cerny that June in which he described his ideas for remaking the Gateway area. A partner in Thorshov and Cerny, one of the city's largest and most successful architectural firms, he was a strong advocate for modern urban planning. Perhaps more important, he was also a go-getter who correctly foresaw big commissions for his firm if the Gateway could be redeveloped. And, by a nice twist of fate, his firm's offices, like those of the HRA, were in the Metropolitan Building.[3]

Cerny's 1945 plan was yet another variant of Jager's 1906 scheme calling for the creation of a new civic center in the Gateway. But Cerny added some distinctly modern touches, most notably a sunken expressway that would cut through

Aerial view of the Gateway area, looking south from near the Mississippi River, 1949. Numerous small buildings still filled many blocks. Gateway Park, near the intersection of Hennepin and Nicollet Avenues, is at lower right.

downtown between Washington Avenue and Third Street. The civic buildings in Cerny's plan were to be located along Third and Fourth Streets and included a new public library, a new federal courthouse, and public health and public safety buildings. Under the plan, much of the rest of the Gateway would be razed to make way for a new industrial district. Although there was little comment about it at the time, the plan was among the first to contemplate demolition of the Metropolitan Building, which stood on the block Cerny had set aside for the new federal courthouse.[4]

A key part of Cerny's plan, the proposed expressway, was never carried out, nor was the bulk of the Gateway turned into an industrial district. But most of the new public buildings he envisioned were, in fact, built. He predicted it would take ten to fifteen years to build them, and this forecast proved to be remarkably accurate. The library, public health building, and federal courthouse were all completed by 1961 and were located almost exactly where Cerny had said they should be. Although these new buildings were not part of the Gateway Center project, they were just outside its boundaries and contributed significantly to the wholesale remaking of the Gateway that began in the late 1950s.

~

As Cerny's plan was unveiled, the *Minneapolis Tribune* and other newspapers continued to push for redevelopment of the Gateway, which was widely seen as a civic embarrassment. By the late 1940s, parts of it had become a full-blown skid row, possibly the largest in any American city with the

exception of the Bowery in New York. The Gateway's population was also aging. In 1920 only about a quarter of the district's residents were over fifty years old. By 1950 the Gateway had turned increasingly gray, and many of its thirty-five hundred or so residents were retired men living on small pensions.[5]

The Gateway's bars, liquor stores, pawnshops, and flophouses occupied buildings that were even more elderly than their clientele and that seemed to become more decrepit with each passing year. A study in the early 1950s identified scores of "obsolete" buildings within the district, particularly along Nicollet, Hennepin, and Washington Avenues. A few structures dated back to the late 1860s and were among the oldest commercial buildings left in the city.

Meanwhile, crime and vice remained persistent problems, and alcohol—the smell of it, the taste of it, the trash from it piled into small mountains of bottles in alleyways and back lots—permeated the district. Yet the Gateway also offered a series of streetscapes, dominated by rows of small brick and stone buildings, that had no equal anywhere else in the city. It was the kind of dense, varied, and organic urban world Jane Jacobs would celebrate in her brilliant 1961 book, *The Death and Life of Great American Cities.* New Orleans had preserved just such a world in its French Quarter, thanks to special legislation approved in the 1930s, but the situation in Minneapolis was much different. By the early 1950s it was clear that Minneapolis civic leaders saw destruction and rebuilding along modern lines as the only way to deal with what was often called the "cancer" of the Gateway.[6]

Rising above this worn but still lively quarter of the city, the Metropolitan Building retained much of its old magnificence. Its walls of green and red stone were perfectly intact, although darkened by decades of coal smoke. Its central court, filled with glowing light, was still the city's great architectural space, and its hydraulic elevators continued their dance through delicate cages of iron, operated by men like Lieue Emond, who celebrated his fifty-fifth year on the job in 1947 and estimated that he traveled eighteen miles up and down every day.[7]

Like most office buildings, the Metropolitan underwent various remodelings over the years. The twelfth floor, where the Guaranty Loan Restaurant had once flourished, was converted to office space, as was the old law library on the tenth

---

Shooting victim at the Minnesotan Hotel, Washington and Second Avenues South, 1950. Crime and vice had long plagued the Gateway, which civic leaders in Minneapolis regarded as a municipal embarrassment.

*"How Sick Is This Heart of Minneapolis?"*

REST ROOMS

PANTHER ROOM

Ground-floor lunchroom, Metropolitan Building, 1959. The Metropolitan was updated over the years with amenities such as the lunchroom, but many of the building's original features remained intact until the very end.

floor. Other offices were refurbished with new fixtures and flooring; a small lunchroom was installed on the first floor, and the old banking halls on the second floor were subdivided. Yet the heart of the building—its magnificent glass-and-iron light court—remained remarkably intact, as did the massive stone exterior.

More important, the building remained economically viable, even if it was no longer downtown's premier business address. In 1946 the building was said to be 98 percent occupied, and it continued to be close to full into the early 1950s, with a roster of tenants that included government agencies such as the HRA, professionals such as Thorshov and Cerny, insurance agencies, and small sales and marketing companies. Even St. Olaf Catholic Church became a temporary tenant after its historic downtown church burned in February 1953. St. Olaf rented a large office space on the second floor and held masses there until 1955, when a new church was completed.[8]

Temporary quarters of St. Olaf Catholic Church, second floor, Metropolitan Building, 1954. St. Olaf's historic downtown church was destroyed by fire in February 1953, and masses were celebrated here until a new church could be built.

By the 1950s the Metropolitan also had new owners. Melvin B. Hansen of Minneapolis and Henry D. Michael of St. Paul bought the building in 1946. The partners, who also owned the Oak Grove Hotel in Minneapolis and other apartments, purchased the building for $450,000 from the Metropolitan Life Insurance Company. The *Minneapolis Times* reported that the partners planned to remodel and modernize the building by, among other things, sandblasting its exterior stone and removing its four rooftop towers. These steps were never taken, however, although Hansen and Michael did make numerous improvements to the building during their fifteen years of ownership.[9]

Hansen would in time become the public face of the partnership when he waged a long and costly campaign to save the building in the late 1950s. Even before that, however, he was well known in Minneapolis for his flamboyant eccentricities. Described by a newspaper columnist as "a large, rollicking roughhouser with rumpled white hair and a history of turmoil," Hansen liked to roam from bar to bar at night, hiring a taxi to transport him, sometimes paying the driver with cuts of choice meat rather than cash. A steady drinker, he went everywhere by taxi. Some of these rides were unusually long. He would regularly hire a taxi to go to the Brainerd area and once supposedly journeyed all the way to Canada by cab to visit a friend's fishing lodge. He favored cowboy apparel, including fringed buckskin jackets and heavy boots, and was even said to carry a lasso now and then.[10]

It appears that Hansen took over day-to-day management of the Metropolitan after the acquisition. He maintained a large office on the top floor, only a few doors down from the quarters of the Minneapolis HRA. Hansen didn't know

Melvin Hansen, 1963. A flamboyant character known for long cab rides and frequent parties, Hansen bought the Metropolitan Building with a partner in 1946. He later fought in court to save the building from destruction.

it, but the building he genuinely seemed to love would, in a matter of a few years, be taken from him by force of law, by the tenant just down the hall.

$\sim$

In 1951 the Minneapolis City Planning Commission ordered a study of the Gateway to determine its potential for redevelopment. The city's planning engineer, Herman Olson, was put in charge of the project, and in February 1952 he released his findings in a document called *A Plan for the Redevelopment of the Lower Loop Area*. Illustrated with numerous maps and charts, it incorporated many of the recommendations in Cerny's 1945 plan, including the expressway. Olson also proposed some new elements, most notably a two-block-long, three-thousand-car parking garage to be built over the expressway between Marquette Avenue and Third Avenue South. The plan went on to suggest, rather oddly, that much of the remade Gateway should be given over to industrial uses. But its most startling feature

Proposed expressway between Washington Avenue and Third Street through the Lower Loop (Gateway area), 1945 and later. The expressway was first suggested in Robert Cerny's 1945 plan, shown here, and was later incorporated into a 1952 city plan that called for demolishing much of the Lower Loop but not the Metropolitan Building.

was the extent of demolition it envisioned, with nearly three hundred buildings identified as candidates for the wrecking ball. The Metropolitan Building, which Olson described as being in good condition, was not among them.[11]

The plan garnered much attention in the local press, where stories about the decaying Gateway had become a regular feature, and was later approved by the city council. Even so, the council had no ready means of implementing the plan, which seemed at first glance like just another of the many dreams that had swirled around the Lower Loop over the years. There was, however, a city agency—the Minneapolis HRA—that stood ready to transform the plan into something concrete.

After its establishment in 1947, the HRA had started slowly, concentrating its attention on the postwar housing shortage. Its first substantial project, in 1950, was the Hi-Lo development, which entailed the construction of nearly one hundred new housing units on a nineteen-acre site in Northeast Minneapolis. Hi-Lo was a city-financed project, but after passage of the 1949 Housing Act, a large pot of federal urban renewal money became available to the HRA, and the agency went after it.[12]

The HRA's first successful effort to win federal funding came in 1956, when it received a $5.6 million grant from the Urban Renewal Administration for the Glenwood housing project in North Minneapolis. By that time, the HRA was well into the process of securing funds for Gateway Center. The agency had begun working on the Gateway in 1953 after receiving Olson's plan. The HRA, however, had to craft a plan of its own that would meet federal requirements, and it undertook a new survey to see if the Gateway was suitable for redevelopment. The agency also needed to establish potential boundaries for redevelopment and to address the sensitive issue of how and where to relocate the district's largely impoverished residents.[13]

The city's newspapers, meanwhile, continued their push for remaking the Gateway while praising the work of the HRA. "If anyone can cut the Gordian knot that has tied up improvements in the Gateway, this [the HRA] is the group that can," a reporter for the *Minneapolis Star* wrote in 1953. So eager was the newspaper for action that another story a few months later carried the headline, "Vital Question of Gateway Project Is 'When Do We Start?' " A smaller heading above read, "Sooner the Better."[14]

As the HRA began laying its plans for the Gateway in 1953, the historic fabric of the district was already beginning to tear. In July the aging Palace Theater, a twenty-four-hundred-seat vaudeville house at 414 Hennepin Avenue, was razed. Two blocks away on Hennepin, Temple Court—the oldest of E. Townsend Mix's buildings in downtown Minneapolis—came down at about the same time. But the most prominent monument to fall in 1953 was the Gateway Pavilion. Tired of maintaining the structure, the Minneapolis Park Board tore it down over the objections of some preservationists. The park itself was swept into the midst of the Gateway Center project, and in the early 1960s it was reconfigured and simplified to the point that it is hard to spot amid the modern-era buildings that now occupy the area.[15]

---

Demolition of Gateway Park Pavilion, 1953. A few years later, many buildings around the park were also demolished as part of the Gateway Center project.

*"How Sick Is This Heart of Minneapolis?"*

In 1954 the HRA's planning for the Gateway took a big step forward when the Housing Act of 1949 was amended to make business and industrial areas eligible for federal urban renewal funds. With a huge potential source of financing now in play, the HRA focused on devising a Gateway plan that would qualify for federal funds. By this time, business owners in the Gateway were already growing nervous, fearing—correctly, as it turned out—that there would be no place for them in the HRA's renewal plan. A group of a hundred business owners went to court in hopes of stopping the HRA's survey of the Gateway, but a judge rejected their case.[16]

The HRA finally issued its preliminary plan in August 1955, and it was quite different from the one prepared three years earlier by the city's planning commission. The HRA plan eliminated the proposed expressway between Third and Fourth Streets, reduced the size of the proposed redevelopment area, and called for new public and office buildings, rather than industrial structures, to fill in much of the Gateway. But like its predecessor, the plan embraced wholesale clearance as its chief redevelopment strategy. Major buildings such as the Great Northern Station, the post office, and the Nicollet Hotel were exempted from the plan, as was the Metropolitan, which was described as being a "useful structure." That judgment would mysteriously change within a few years, when the HRA decided the building was obsolete and had to be removed.[17]

Most major American cities undertook large-scale urban renewal projects in the period from 1945 to the mid-1960s. Boston tore up its historic West End, Pittsburgh rebuilt a big chunk of its downtown (as part of a project that was also called Gateway Center), Chicago cleared away old neighborhoods to create thousands of new high-rise apartments. What these projects had in common was an attack on "blight," a deeply loaded word that held an almost mythic significance for urban planners. Blight was a creeping, cancerous thing that threatened the very well-being of cities, and only by excising it in the way a surgeon might remove a tumor could the urban patient be restored to good health. The word was built into the language of the Housing Act of 1949, and no news story on urban renewal was complete without it.[18]

Yet it was a slippery term, and almost any neighborhood of old and less than impeccably maintained buildings might qualify in the eyes of planners as a blighted area. In the case of the Gateway, the word was especially tricky to apply because the age, condition, and use of buildings varied widely. Although there were standards for determining the existence of blight within a given area, the word was elastic enough to cause confusion and uncertainty. A *Minneapolis Star* story in 1959 brought the point home, describing how the HRA and another agency met to "discuss blight and speed up efforts to combat it," only to be "stymied on a question of just what blight is." Despite such doubts, "blight" remained perhaps the most powerful word in the vocabulary of urban renewal, and efforts to remove it inspired massive projects in cities around the country.[19]

Blight, however, was not a term that could readily be applied to the Metropolitan Building. While it was certainly old, the building in the 1950s was by no stretch of the imagination a blighted, poorly kept property. Instead, another argument—that it was functionally obsolete—was trotted out to justify its destruction.

Obsolescence by the 1950s had a fairly well-defined meaning as applied to office buildings like the Metropolitan. As early as 1922, a study undertaken for the National Association of Building Owners and Managers (NABOM) concluded that office buildings typically had a productive life of just twenty-eight years. After that, they supposedly became functionally obsolete as newer buildings offered better office space and more amenities. Even a building that was fully occupied and well maintained could not avoid becoming obsolete, or so the study suggested. It was a handy idea, particularly because it gave owners another way to write down taxes as buildings aged, and it gained widespread acceptance.[20]

By the 1950s, the Metropolitan Building may indeed have been obsolete by NABOM's standards, but it was in fact still perfectly functional, as its high occupancy rate demonstrated. NABOM's study was done in Chicago, a city so notorious for demolition fever that at one point the average life span of downtown office buildings there was a mere thirty-two years. In most other American cities, however, office buildings typically survived for a much longer time. This is certainly true in downtown Minneapolis, where at least ten sizable office buildings that are more than one hundred years old still stand, led by the redoubtable Lumber Exchange, which dates to 1886. The Metropolitan, had the HRA simply left it alone, would almost surely be part of that group today.[21]

$\sim$

The HRA formally approved its initial Gateway plan in 1956, a year in which forces that would bring enormous changes to downtown Minneapolis began to coalesce rapidly. In March the HRA won a $50,000 grant from the federal Urban Renewal Administration to undertake additional planning for the Gateway. That same month, the state Highway Department unveiled plans showing how the new interstate system would sweep around the edges of downtown, leaving a wide swath of destruction in its wake. In July came word that most of the block on which the Metropolitan Building stood would be razed to make way for a new federal courthouse.[22]

There was at this time a palpable sense of urgency in Minneapolis about the need for downtown renewal, much of it driven by a fear of suburban growth that seemed to threaten the very future of the city. By the 1950s the great rush to suburbia was in full swing, and Minneapolis for the first time in its history began losing population as new subdivisions spread with stunning speed across the flatlands of Richfield, Bloomington, and Brooklyn Center. As the suburbs mushroomed, business owners worked to rid downtown of its rather antique aura by applying modern facelifts to scores of historic storefronts and buildings. Even some of downtown's largest Victorians, including the 1883 Syndicate Block and Donaldson's 1888 Glass Block, disappeared behind new, simplified facades that sought to cleanse them of their messy old architectural details.[23]

There were other changes as well. In 1951 the first two modern-style parking ramps appeared in the downtown core. More would quickly follow, even as traffic jams became a regular occurrence. One-way streets were soon introduced in hopes of reducing congestion, but they did not prove to be a panacea. In 1954 the last streetcar rolled through downtown as buses took over the job of public transportation. Almost everywhere downtown, or so it seemed, the new was sweeping out the old, but it was not enough.

In 1955 came the disheartening news that General Mills, which had once maintained its corporate offices in the Metropolitan Building, was leaving downtown to build a new headquarters complex in Golden Valley. A year later, in October 1956, another threat to downtown's hegemony appeared in Edina when Southdale Center—the nation's first fully enclosed suburban shopping mall—opened its doors to huge crowds and ecstatic reviews.[24]

In a guest editorial written for the *Minneapolis Star* in July 1955, Robert Cerny—who continued to promote clearance of the Gateway as vigorously as ever—offered

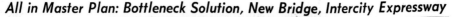

## All in Master Plan: Bottleneck Solution, New Bridge, Intercity Expressway

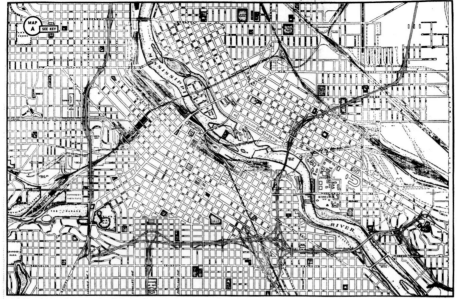

Map showing proposed routes of freeways around downtown Minneapolis, 1956. Hundreds of buildings were demolished to make way for the freeways, which were being built just as the Gateway Center project was transforming a large portion of downtown.

a stark assessment of the impact of suburban growth. "For the first time the city faces competition for people, for homes, for stores and for factories," he wrote, noting that new shopping centers like Southdale posed a particular threat. He argued that Minneapolis, "for the good of itself and the metropolitan area," had to make bold plans to combat the rising power of the suburbs, beginning with redevelopment of the Gateway. Cerny went on to paint a grim picture of how blight could easily spread south from the Gateway toward Sixth Street, threatening the heart of downtown. He also argued, as did the HRA, that redeveloping the Gateway would significantly improve the city's property tax base.[25]

Cerny's alarmist language was echoed in numerous newspaper stories. Both the *Star* and *Tribune* published frequent articles bemoaning the rundown condition of the Gateway and pushing for its complete redevelopment. "How sick is this heart of Minneapolis today?" the *Tribune* asked in a story in January 1956. The answer, according to the article, was that the patient was very old, very unkempt,

Last run of Minneapolis streetcars along Hennepin Avenue, June 19, 1954. Buses replaced the streetcars, which had been a fixture of life in the city since 1889. It would be fifty years before light-rail transit returned to Minneapolis.

very fond of alcohol, and therefore very ill. Using data from the latest city studies, the story noted that 77 percent of the buildings in the Gateway were constructed before 1895, 70 percent had received no major repairs since 1920, and 48 percent were located within a block of a bar or liquor store. The story's clear message—that the Gateway was an alcohol-soaked dive of a neighborhood—would be repeated time and again as pressure built to clear it all away.[26]

The *Tribune*'s story was exaggerated—parts of the Gateway remained economically viable and its stock of buildings included many solid structures like the Metropolitan—but there was also much truth in it. The Gateway was indeed burdened with many decrepit buildings, it did have significant social problems related to alcohol and poverty, and many of its residents lived in grossly substandard housing. In another time, an integrated approach to revitalizing the Gateway that included selective demolition along with rehabilitation and reuse of its best buildings might have resulted in a vibrant transformation. But in the 1950s, well before historic preservation laws and historic tax credits came into being, there was no public mechanism to undertake such a course, nor was there any real possibility of extensive privately financed redevelopment along such lines.

Instead, the city and its HRA faced what appeared to be a stark choice: either mow down the Gateway with the aid of millions in federal dollars or do nothing and possibly allow the district's cancerous rot to spread, as Cerny and others predicted it would. The choice seemed obvious, and it wouldn't be long before the historic Gateway was doomed.

The fate of the Metropolitan Building, meanwhile, remained very much in the balance. The HRA's 1956 Gateway plan did not call for the building's destruction. But as the agency continued to revise its plans in hopes of qualifying for federal aid, a different picture began to emerge. In March 1957 the *Minneapolis Star* published a story and map suggesting the Metropolitan Building was still exempt from demolition in the HRA's latest plan. Just a month later, however, the newspaper offered contradictory information in a rhapsodic article by two reporters envisioning what a new "Golden Gateway" might look like in 1967. "Look beyond, across Hennepin Avenue and you see the fresh, new buildings of the Golden Gateway," the reporters wrote. "We used to call it the lower loop—remember? The name vanished with the blight." So, too, according to the story, did the Metropolitan Building, described as an old "castle" that had been replaced by a new Veterans Building and government plaza.[27]

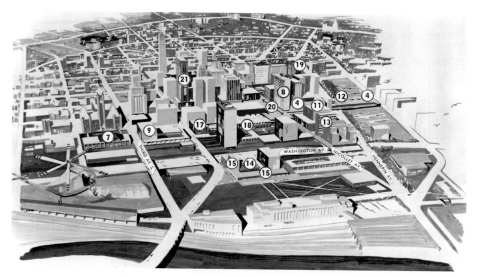

Bird's-eye view of "Golden Gateway," 1957. The new Gateway was supposed to be a wondrous place, bright and modern, but what was actually built rarely turned out to be impressive. Key: 4 transportation center (proposed), 7 state office building (proposed), 8 Sheraton–Hilton Hotel (proposed), 9 public health building (proposed), 11 library (proposed), 12 heliport (proposed), 13 Nicollet Hotel, 14 Labor Plaza (proposed), 15 Minnesotan Hotel, 17 veterans building (proposed), 18 federal courts building (proposed), 19 hotel, 20 Nicollet Plaza (proposed), 21 First National Bank (proposed).

Although neither the Veterans Building nor the plaza ever materialized, the *Star* story and others over the next few months left little doubt that the Metropolitan Building, contrary to earlier plans, was being targeted by the HRA for demolition. Exactly how and when this happened is difficult to comprehend. The minutes of the regular meetings of the HRA's five-member board during this period appear to have been lost, and there was little newspaper coverage of the board's deliberations. But in its annual report for 1957, the agency included a map indicating the Metropolitan would be removed, along with approximately two hundred other buildings in the Gateway. The report provided no insight into why the agency had decided to include the Metropolitan in the zone of destruction. It was only after the plan to demolish the building encountered fierce resistance, beginning in 1958, that the HRA and its executive director, Robert Jorvig, began to offer a series of explanations—none very convincing—for why the Metropolitan had to be taken down.

A Harvard-trained planner, Jorvig was highly regarded in the profession and would later go on to become the first executive director of the Metropolitan Council, the Twin Cities' regional planning agency. He took the job in Minneapolis in 1956 after serving three years as head of St. Paul's HRA. Jorvig proved to be an effective leader, and under his direction planning for what would become the Gateway Center project moved forward at a steady pace. In July 1957 the federal Urban Renewal Administration agreed to provide up to $14 million in funding for the project. Two months later, the federal agency gave preliminary approval to the HRA's plan after slightly modifying the boundaries of the renewal area. Final federal approval came on May 22, 1958. The

Robert Jorvig, circa 1960. A Harvard-trained planner, Jorvig took over as executive director of the Minneapolis Housing and Redevelopment Authority in 1956. He led the way in developing and promoting the Gateway Center project.

Gateway, the decaying old soul of Minneapolis that had inspired dreams of renewal for a half century, was about to be swept away, as was its greatest monument.[28]

Six days later, the Minneapolis City Planning Commission and the HRA approved the plan, but with one dissenting voice. The dissenter, who served on the commission, was Ralph Rapson, dean of the University of Minnesota's School of Architecture and one of the state's leading modernist architects. Although Rapson supported the Gateway Center project as a whole, he thought the Metropolitan Building should be preserved and so abstained from casting a vote. "It makes me very sad to see the building go," he said. "It is the only real architectural monument we have in this area."[29]

The same newspaper story in which Rapson was quoted also offered what may have been Jorvig's first public defense of the HRA's decision to tear down the Metropolitan. He said that after "lengthy consideration" the HRA determined that the building needed "costly repair and modernization which would not permit it to compete economically with new office buildings scheduled to rise in the lower loop." This argument was dubious at best. The Metropolitan was a well-occupied, structurally sound, fully functional office building that in fact would not have competed with the single-user buildings that later rose as part of the Gateway project. As time went on, Jorvig and the HRA would offer up other arguments as well, most of which were readily countered, to no avail, by the building's many defenders.

~

As finally approved by a unanimous vote of the Minneapolis City Council in 1958, the Lower Loop redevelopment plan, which was soon renamed Gateway Center, was the largest federally financed downtown urban renewal project, in terms of area, ever undertaken in the United States. The project encompassed 68.1 acres spread across fifteen entire blocks and parts of seven others. Its boundaries extended from First Avenue North to Fifth Avenue South and from First to Fifth Streets. About half the project area was taken up by streets and alleys, leaving 35.5 acres for potential redevelopment. The federal government ultimately put about $13.5 million into the project, with the city providing another $4 million, to acquire and raze 212 buildings, of which the Metropolitan was by far the best known.[30]

The boundaries were carefully, if quite arbitrarily, drawn. The Lumber Exchange, for example, was left just outside the project area, even though it was four years older than the Metropolitan and in similar condition. In later court testimony, Jorvig suggested it might have cost too much money to acquire and raze the Lumber Exchange, so it was omitted from the project. Yet the Metropolitan was also a very costly proposition for the HRA, which ultimately spent nearly $900,000 to acquire and demolish the building. The agency also racked up thousands of dollars in legal fees to defend its actions in court.

Within the final Gateway project boundaries there were also a number of excluded sites that reflected special circumstances. The entire block bound by Third and Fourth Streets and Nicollet and Hennepin Avenues was left out because all its buildings were about to be razed to make way for the new Minneapolis Central Library. The Nicollet Hotel was also excluded, as was most of a block directly to the east of the Metropolitan that included the new Public Health Building, completed in 1957, and the soon-to-be-constructed State Employment Security Building. Much of the block on which the Metropolitan stood also fell in the exempt category because of plans to build a new federal courthouse there.

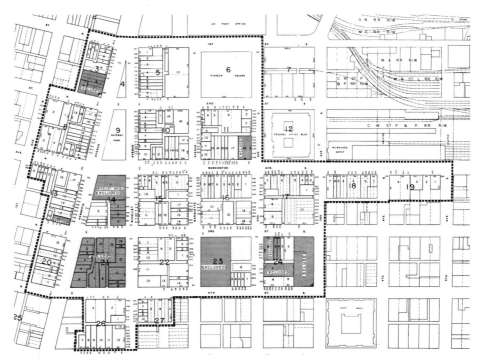

Map of Gateway Center urban renewal area, 1958. More than two hundred buildings spread across twenty-two blocks were slated for demolition as part of the Gateway Center project, which the Minneapolis City Council approved by a unanimous vote in 1958.

The massive program of demolition that formed the basis of the Gateway Project sparked little controversy at first. After one public hearing, the *Tribune* noted, "not a voice was raised against the basic redevelopment plan for the Minneapolis Lower Loop." Instead, debate centered on the fate of the three thousand people, mostly older men, who would be displaced by the project.[31]

The city and HRA initially floated the idea of building new public housing for the displaced residents in an area along Washington Avenue North. This proposal, however, drew heated opposition from nearby business owners. The city council, after a series of public hearings, ultimately voted against the public housing plan, and in the end the Gateway's residents were simply dispersed to other housing units around the city. In most cases, these new accommodations proved much better than the old ones, although some relocated residents complained that they missed the Gateway's dense, busy environment.[32]

When the Gateway Center plan became public, newspaper stories made it clear that the Metropolitan Building faced demolition. Even so, there seems to have been little initial reaction to this news from preservationists or the public at large, although the building's owners, led by Melvin Hansen, fought the idea from the start in meetings with the HRA. It wasn't until late October 1958, when the HRA moved to condemn the Metropolitan, that a campaign began to save the building.

It would be the first great historic preservation battle in state history and it would rage for nearly two years amid a welter of claims and counterclaims, endorsements from some of the nation's leading architects and historians, lawsuits, and even dark allegations of conspiracy and fraud. Through it all, the HRA remained implacable, so much so that it is hard not to conclude from the historic record that the Metropolitan never stood a chance.

# 8

# "A Monstrosity in the Eyes of Most Observers"

On October 30, 1958, as the final version of the Gateway Center plan neared approval, the *Minneapolis Star*, for perhaps the first time, raised an objection. The newspaper had long supported the idea of redeveloping the Gateway, and would continue to do so, but now there was a caveat, and it centered on the Metropolitan Building. Describing the building as "a landmark dear to many citizens," the *Star* wrote, "it is still useful as an office structure. The building which would replace it might not be nearly so attractive." Although the editorial was hardly a denunciation of the HRA's plan—the writer assured readers that the newspaper did not want "to embarrass the redevelopment authority in its splendid work"—it marked the beginning of what would be a long fight to save the building.[1]

In its scope and duration, the battle over the building was unprecedented in Minneapolis. Like virtually every other American city, Minneapolis by the 1950s had already experienced numerous cycles of demolition and rebuilding in and around its downtown. Other than an occasional lament in the newspapers, buildings—even prominent ones—usually came down without much public notice, and organized preservation campaigns were unheard of. This was true right up to the time of the big battle over the Metropolitan.

---

Remains of the old U.S. Post Office, at Third Street and Marquette Avenue, seen through a window of the Metropolitan Building, 1961. The post office was demolished after a new and remarkably unattractive federal courthouse opened on the same block.

In 1958, for instance, the ten-story New York Life Building at Fifth Street and Second Avenue South, just two blocks from the Metropolitan, was demolished to make way for a new twenty-eight-story skyscraper for the First National Bank. Constructed in 1890, the New York Life included a stunning skylit lobby and was one of downtown's most significant historic buildings, yet its destruction drew hardly any notice in the press. The demolition in 1960 of the old U.S. Post Office next door to the Metropolitan also failed to stir much interest.[2]

The fact that the Metropolitan Building, unlike so many others, inspired a preservation battle stemmed from both its high standing as a work of architecture and the willingness of its owners, especially Melvin Hansen, to put up a fight. Hansen's motives were mixed. It appears he truly cherished the building and believed it should be preserved, but he was also deeply dissatisfied with the price offered by the HRA for the building. He eventually took his claim, with little success, all the way to the Minnesota Supreme Court.

∼

When the news that the Metropolitan Building was slated for demolition finally began to sink in, it drew an immediate response, largely in the form of letters to the editor published in the Minneapolis newspapers. The letters of protest came from architects, historians, and the public at large. There was even a letter from a writer who identified himself as Frank L. Wright, which must have caused a bit of a stir, if only because it appeared two years after the legendary architect's death. The writers all made similar arguments: the Metropolitan was a unique and dazzling work of architecture, it was still viable as an office building, and there was simply no reason it had to be demolished. These arguments were sound, but they did nothing to sway the HRA, which never deviated from its plan to tear down the building.[3]

In February 1959, just days before the Lower Loop project was officially renamed the Gateway Center Urban Renewal Plan, the HRA made its initial offer of $587,500 for the Metropolitan Building. Although the offer was well above the building's assessed valuation of $222,500, Hansen and his co-owners, who by this time included not only Henry Michael but also his son James, quickly rejected the offer as far too low. They also argued, as they had all along, that the building should be exempted from the Gateway Center plan. The *Minneapolis Star* reported two months later that the building might even "get a reprieve from its death sentence" because Hansen and Michael had offered to hire an architect to "draw up a plan to rehabilitate the Met and make it serviceable for some time to come." The story went on to quote James Michael as saying, "We've already spent a million dollars in improvements and we'll spend more."[4]

Jorvig and the HRA, however, do not appear to have taken the owners' offer seriously. Instead, in an interview with the *Star*, Jorvig insisted that only a long list of extremely costly improvements, such as replacing the entire skylight over the light court, could save the building from the wrecker. He also claimed that the Metropolitan presented a hazard to the public because of loose exterior stonework, even though there was no evidence that anything had ever fallen off the building.[5]

Robert Cerny was among those drawn into the debate over the Metropolitan's future. From his offices on the fourth floor of the building, the architect suggested in a letter to the *Minneapolis Tribune* in December 1958 that the only way to save the Metropolitan would be through a public funding program similar to those by which European governments maintained important monuments. It was nice idea, and one that would by the 1970s find its way into American public policy through tax credits for historic preservation and other programs, but it had little practical application at the time, as Cerny surely knew. Cerny went on to contend that the HRA was not to blame for "destroying" the Metropolitan. Rather, he said, the building "has lived its economic life and cannot survive without a substantial transfusion." It was a disingenuous argument at best. The Metropolitan was in fact in no worse condition than other downtown Minneapolis office buildings of similar age, and with basic improvements it could have survived quite nicely for years to come, if only the HRA had left it alone.[6]

But the agency, as Jorvig had made clear, was not inclined to do so, and its policies stacked the deck against the Metropolitan from the start. The HRA had developed a set of standards for buildings within Gateway Center and it took the position that the seventy-year-old Metropolitan would have to meet these criteria, even though they were designed to apply to new buildings within the project area. There was, for example, a standard requiring all new buildings to be set back from the street behind open plazas. The Metropolitan clearly could not meet this requirement, nor could it possibly adhere to all the provisions of modern building codes. Even so, the HRA continued to insist, in catch-22 fashion, that the building had to be demolished because it could not meet a set of unattainable ideals the agency itself had established.

In June 1959 the fight on behalf of the building gained momentum with the formation of a Save the Met Committee led by the Hennepin County Historical Society. The Minnesota Historical Society also joined the fray. Meanwhile, attorneys for Hansen and the Michaels met at least three times with Jorvig and others members of the HRA's staff to make their case for saving the building. These meetings produced no change in the HRA's position, however, and the debate over the building continued to roil in the newspapers.[7]

Two of the committee's most active members were Edward V. Loftstrom and Walter H. Wheeler, both longtime tenants of the Metropolitan. Lofstrom, an architect, challenged many of the HRA's statements regarding the condition of the building. "If the Metropolitan is out-of-date by today's standards," he wrote in one letter to the *Tribune*, "so are 90 per cent of the buildings in Minneapolis. Shall we tear them all down?" He also noted, as did many others who argued on behalf of the building, that it could be brought up to modern standards "for a fraction of the cost of providing equivalent space in a new building."[8]

Wheeler was equally tenacious in defending the Metropolitan. A nationally recognized structural engineer whose superb Mendota Bridge (1925) remains a prominent Twin Cities landmark, Wheeler knew the building as well as anyone. He'd maintained his offices on the eighth floor since 1916 and was probably the building's longest-standing tenant by 1959. Well into his seventies but still working, Wheeler was outraged by the idea of destroying what he called "an irreplaceable example of American architecture." A rock-ribbed conservative, he also objected to what he saw as a great waste of public funds to acquire and raze a perfectly sound building.[9]

Over a span of two years, Wheeler did everything in his power to save the Metropolitan. He wrote numerous letters in support of its preservation to the *Star* and *Tribune* and to every public official he could think of, including Minneapolis mayor P. K. Peterson and Minnesota's two U.S. senators at the time, Hubert Humphrey and Eugene McCarthy. In a typically strong letter to Peterson in July 1959, Wheeler dismissed as "veritable nonsense" the notion that the Metropolitan was a "blighted building" or that it was in a "blighted district." But his letters had little effect. Wheeler also testified for the building's owners in their court case against the HRA and pointedly rebutted the agency's contention that the building was obsolete and a potential firetrap. As the hour grew desperate, he even hired a private detective to dig into the possibility that city and HRA officials had accepted bribes, although there was nothing to support such suspicions.[10]

Despite his obvious love for the Metropolitan, Wheeler seems to have labored under a major misconception regarding its history. In several documents he attributed the building to an old friend of his, Minneapolis architect Leroy Buffington (1847–1931). Wheeler's confusion may have arisen from the fact that Buffington had designed the nearby Boston Block at Third Street and Hennepin Avenue. That building, razed in 1942–43, contained a light court nearly as large as the Metropolitan's. Although Wheeler's history was a bit shaky, his defense of the Metropolitan was consistently strong and

Walter Wheeler, circa 1932. A highly regarded structural engineer, Wheeler maintained his offices in the Metropolitan Building for more than forty years and was a strong advocate for its preservation.

intelligent, and no one did a better job of challenging the HRA's highly questionable claims regarding the condition of the building.

~

The agitation surrounding the HRA's plan to demolish the Metropolitan compelled the agency in 1959 to undertake a new study of the building to assess its condition. A. C. Godward, a consulting engineer who had served as the agency's director before Jorvig took over in 1956, was put in charge of the study. Godward concluded the building needed $1 million or more in improvements, including possible enclosure of the light court with wire glass as a fire safety measure. Although Godward recommended demolishing the Metropolitan, he said that with more limited improvements it could go on as what he described as a "Class Four" office building.[11]

Some of Godward's findings were hotly disputed—Wheeler, for one, said there was no need to enclose the light court—but in September 1959 the five-member HRA board voted unanimously to reaffirm its decision to condemn the Metropolitan. Any effort to modernize the building, the board said, would require "expenditures which could not be recaptured in the competitive market." The board also made the patently false claim, based on unfounded fears of falling stonework, that if left standing the building "would soon require demolition in the interests of public safety."[12]

～

As the debate over the Metropolitan grew ever more fractious, the HRA in late 1959 put the Gateway Center project in motion, amid much eager coverage in the press. The old Vendome Hotel at 19–23 Fourth Street South was the first building to be torn down. Featuring a carved version of the Statue of Liberty's head mounted on a rooftop pediment, the five-story building offered one of downtown's most elaborately finished facades, with much fine detailing in white stone. The hotel, largely rebuilt after a 1902 fire, had 250 rooms, the best cigar shop in the city, but no bar (the owners were teetotalers). The equally old Milner (originally Rogers) Hotel soon came down as well, and by 1960 wrecking balls were busily at work throughout the Lower Loop.[13]

By the time the campaign of destruction began in the Gateway, the courts had already cleared the way for the HRA to act. One of the most important cases actually occurred in St. Paul, where seventy-four downtown property owners sued that city's HRA over a plan to acquire and redevelop land for a new Sears, Roebuck and Company store near the capitol. The property owners challenged the legality of the state's Municipal Housing and Redevelopment Act of 1947, under which the HRA was empowered to condemn and remove blighted properties. But in June 1959 a Ramsey District Court judge ruled the 1947 law was constitutional and the Sears project could proceed.[14]

In Minneapolis, the owners of Schiek's Café, which had been located on Third

_____

Vendome Hotel, Fourth Street between Hennepin and Nicollet Avenues, circa 1915. The old hotel, which featured a rooftop replica of the Statue of Liberty's head, was the first building to be demolished for the Gateway Center project. It was gone by early 1960.

*"A Monstrosity in the Eyes of Most Observers"*

Schiek's Café, circa 1900. The luxurious old café on Third Street at Nicollet Avenue was condemned as part of the Gateway Center project. The owners fought condemnation in court but lost, and the café was razed in 1961.

Street South near Nicollet Avenue since 1912, filed one of the first lawsuits against the Gateway Center project in the summer of 1959. The suit claimed, among other things, that the HRA's plan to demolish the café was arbitrary and capricious because it was not a "blighted" property in any sense of the term. That argument failed to persuade Hennepin District Court judge Harold N. Rogers, who ruled in favor of the HRA in October. Two months later, Rogers took on the much bigger case of the Metropolitan Building.[15]

After failing to convince the HRA to leave the Metropolitan out of Gateway Center, Hansen and Michael filed what would be the first of several lawsuits in hopes of saving the building. The suit was filed in October 1959 after the HRA gave notice of its intent to condemn the Metropolitan. As was true of the Schiek's case, the main issue centered on whether the HRA had acted arbitrarily.

The building's condition became a key point of contention during the trial before Rogers in December. A half-dozen witnesses testified for the HRA, including city fire and elevator inspectors, and they all described the building as little more than a disaster waiting to happen. Some of the most negative testimony came from a deputy Minneapolis building inspector named James T. Ostrow, who went out of his way to depict the Metropolitan as decrepit and all but impossible to renovate. He even suggested, absurdly, that all of its stone walls would have to be replaced in order to make it safe.[16]

Walter Wheeler, who would later ascribe Ostrow's testimony to "his *ignorance* of the facts and also his prejudice," took the stand to counter the building inspector's ridiculously alarmist claims. The Metropolitan, he said, was in solid structural condition, posed no safety threat to the public, and did not require, as Ostrow contended, drastic and extremely expensive renovations. Hansen also testified, estimating that it would cost no more than $600,000 to upgrade the building, an investment he said could be recouped by raising rents.[17]

But it was Robert Jorvig, the HRA's director, who provided perhaps the most telling testimony of all. At several points during his questioning, Jorvig pointed to what may have been the decisive factor—aesthetics—behind the HRA's insistence on demolishing the Metropolitan. He said the building was a sore thumb that, if allowed to stand, would not only be out of place in the new Gateway Center but also might even discourage development nearby. "It is an old building," he testified, "and it is located well within the project boundaries and would be one of the dominant buildings if it were left, and the old architecture and condition of the building, in our opinion, would deter adjoining investment of any substantial size."[18]

Over the next two years, the HRA would make this argument time and again, dismissing the Metropolitan as a giant Victorian eyesore that could scare off anyone planning to build a modern, and presumably much more attractive, building nearby. In a 2001 interview, long after his retirement, Jorvig claimed that businesses thinking about building in the new Gateway wanted all of its old structures, including the Metropolitan, to come down. "It was tough to get people to invest in that area with the history it had," he said. "They were really concerned that you weren't going to provide them with a nice block of property with a whole lot of blight around it."[19]

The Sheraton-Ritz hotel chain and IBM were among the large companies that ended up building in the new Gateway. According to the HRA, both insisted on

A sign along Third Street advertising the Gateway Center project, circa 1960. The Metropolitan Building, slightly out of focus, looms in the background, looking a bit like the ghost it will soon become.

contract language calling for the Metropolitan to be removed, not only because of its old-fashioned appearance but also out of fear such a supposedly decrepit building would depress surrounding property values. Yet when members of the Save the Met Committee contacted the two companies, both firmly denied that they had ever demanded the Metropolitan's destruction.[20]

Although the companies may have said one thing in public and quite another in private to the HRA, there's no proof the Metropolitan ever posed a threat to redevelopment in the Gateway area. Even so, Jorvig and the HRA clearly viewed the building as an ugly, anachronistic intruder with the potential to disturb their modernist dreams of a shining new Gateway. Their attitude was summed up in a letter the HRA's attorney, Ben Palmer, later wrote to the *Star*. Noting with disapproval that the building possessed such out-of-date features as "ornament, bay windows and round towers on all four corners," he asserted that the Metropolitan was nothing less than "a monstrosity in the eyes of most observers."[21]

While Palmer may not have endeared himself to the public with his remarks about the building, he won his case in court. On December 21, 1959, Judge Rogers ruled the HRA had the legal right to condemn the Metropolitan. Obviously swayed by Ostrow's damning testimony, Rogers wrote in a memorandum that the Metropolitan was a "blighted"' building and was "unsafe both on the exterior and interior for continued occupancy and use. It is further clear that the necessary repairs, if they could be made, to put the building in safe condition, would not place the building in such shape that it would be a proper part of the projected new development, and the expenditures to completely modernize it would apparently be economically unsound."[22]

Rogers's ruling was a complete victory for the HRA and also a death warrant for the Metropolitan. Hansen and Michael appealed the decision to the Minnesota Supreme Court, but that body was no more inclined than Rogers to challenge the HRA's version of the facts or to find that its actions were arbitrary and capricious. In a decision issued on August 5, 1960, the high court upheld Rogers while describing the Metropolitan as an "architectural anachronism." The court went on to say, "It seems clear that the building is indisputably out of date and would to some extent be out of place in the project area."[23]

∽

The supreme court's decision came, suitably enough, at the beginning of what was to be the most transformative decade in downtown Minneapolis since the 1880s. So much work was under way in so many places by the early 1960s that downtown became the whirling center of a vast dance of destruction. Wrecking balls gnawed at the Gateway through 1963, while scores of other downtown buildings, including most of the remaining historic mansions, fell to make way for one new project or another, or simply to become parking lots.

Meanwhile, on the edges of downtown, the way was being cleared for Interstates 94 and 35W. By one estimate, as many as seventy-five hundred people were displaced for the new freeways, which tore through an old apartment and rooming house district, leaving behind a wide swath of demolished buildings. An entire street—Forest Avenue, just south of Groveland Avenue on the flanks of Lowry Hill—was eliminated to make room for the freeways, and with it went more than twenty homes and apartment buildings. All told, at least five hundred

(*Above*) Demolition of the Phoenix Building, north on Marquette Avenue from Fourth Street, 1961. The soon-to-be-razed Palace Building at Fourth Street and Nicollet Avenue is at left. To the right is the recently completed U.S. Courthouse. (*Right*) Aerial view of cleared Gateway, south from above Mississippi River, 1962. The Metropolitan Building is already gone. A few new buildings, including the Sheraton-Ritz Hotel at Third Street and Nicollet Avenue, have begun to rise amid the sea of parking lots.

structures in and around downtown Minneapolis were razed in the 1960s, including the two hundred that came down for Gateway Center.[24]

When the Gateway Center plan was formally unveiled to the public in 1959, the newspapers presented it as a magnificent new urban world that would be filled with elegant modern buildings and many amenities. This did not turn out to be the case. The first new buildings to appear in the Gateway were public in nature. By 1961 there were four—the Central Library, the U.S. Courthouse, the Public Health Building, and the State Employment Security Building. None offered memorable architecture, and one of them—the federal courthouse designed by Cerny's firm and located next to the Metropolitan Building—was unbelievably banal. The most important new work of public architecture that touched on

the Gateway area was Nicollet Mall, completed in 1967, but it wasn't actually part of the renewal project.

Private development in Gateway Center began in 1961, when the Knutson Company, a Minneapolis development firm, paid $5.9 million for much of the land being cleared by the HRA. Knutson's development efforts, however, did not proceed as rapidly as anticipated, and some sites remained empty for twenty years or more. A number of grand schemes that might have enlivened the district also failed to materialize. Among them was Scandia, a large complex Knutson hoped to develop along Nicollet Avenue between Second Street and Washington Avenue. The block-square project was supposed to include offices for Scandinavian consulates as well as restaurants and a skating rink, all arranged around a sunken plaza. It was an intriguing idea, but Knutson was never able to make it happen.[25]

In the end, the redeveloped Gateway turned out to be far short of the gleaming modernist paradise depicted by the newspapers, despite Knutson's claim that the rebuilt district was "the showpiece of a dynamic city." With the delightful exception of Minoru Yamasaki's Northwestern National Life Insurance Building (1964), most of the new architecture was remarkable only for its dullness. One of the most ballyhooed projects was the Sheraton-Ritz Hotel, which opened at 315 Nicollet Avenue in 1963. Designed by Cerny's firm, the seventeen-story, three-hundred-room luxury hotel was billed, with a comic level of hyperbole, as a small version of Rockefeller Center in New York. But aside from a jazzy parking ramp, the hotel was a bland affair, and it survived for only twenty-seven years before being wrecked. A nearby six-story building for the IBM Corporation, constructed in 1962, had an even shorter life, standing for just twenty-three years.[26]

George Nelson, one of the leading designers of the midcentury era, visited the new Gateway late in 1962 and was not impressed by what he saw. "It seems to lack unity," he said. "The buildings are not necessarily bad individually, but they really don't have a great deal to do with one another. . . . As a result you get a kind of anarchy in a situation that pretends to have order."

Nelson's comments were well taken. As Gateway Center slowly filled in with new buildings, the once crowded district acquired a coldly minimalist look, with isolated buildings set like abstract sculptures amid plazas and parking lots. To anyone familiar with the old Gateway, it must have seemed as though the vital spark of life had been extinguished from the place under the bleak banner of

Sheraton-Ritz Hotel, west on Third Street toward Marquette Avenue, 1966. The luxury hotel was likened by one company official to Rockefeller Center in New York, a comparison that could not be described as apt. Never a great success, the hotel was torn down in 1990.

modernization. Perhaps the renewed Gateway's greatest success, in the end, was as a generator of increased property taxes for the city.[27]

~

Although the supreme court's ruling left little doubt that the Metropolitan was headed for demolition, its many admirers kept up the fight to preserve it, hoping that the only real power they had—the power of persuasion—might somehow win the day. The HRA, however, gave no evidence that it was about to change its mind. As if to underscore its position, the agency in April 1960 moved its offices out of the building, a none-too-subtle statement that it considered the Metropolitan to be doomed. Even so, Hansen in particular intensified his efforts on behalf of the building. He gave colorful interviews to the newspapers, orchestrated a letter-writing campaign, and staged a Save the Met rally in front of the building that included a horse-drawn buggy and women dressed in Victorian-era clothes.[28]

(*Previous spread*) Gateway area, southeast from near First Street and First Avenue North, 1968. New buildings, such as the River Towers Condominiums (left center) and the Northwestern National Life Insurance Building (right center), quickly filled in some of the blocks cleared for Gateway Center. Others remained parking lots for years.

———————————

The protests grew more urgent in 1961 as the HRA moved to condemn the building and clear out its tenants. Although the *Star* and *Tribune* gave plenty of publicity to the Save the Met campaign, and several prominent columnists bemoaned what was about to happen, the newspapers' editorial pages backed the HRA. One *Star* editorial expressed regret over the building's impending destruction but said it would be a worthy trade-off since a redeveloped Gateway "offers promise of a new civic era in which blight gives way to beauty, spaciousness and order." If that turned out to be a pipe dream, it was a dream nevertheless shared by the city's civic and business leaders, and in such an environment the Metropolitan had no chance of surviving once the courts had ruled in the HRA's favor.[29]

Hansen, Wheeler, and others refused to give up the fight, however. In early 1961 Wheeler sent out a new blitz of letters to public officials. The response he received from Senator Hubert Humphrey was typical. "While I sympathize with you wholeheartedly in your desire to continue this building [the Met]," Humphrey wrote, "the inclusion of one building or another is wholly within the province of local government." By the summer of 1961, Wheeler's anger had congealed into the hard mush of conspiracy theory, and he paid a three-hundred-dollar retainer to hire a private detective named Frank J. Dunleavy to investigate the HRA and others he suspected of criminal wrongdoing in connection with the Gateway Center project. "The whole thing seems to me to have a bad smell and especially the determination to remove the Metropolitan Building," Wheeler wrote to Dunleavy in June. But even if the detective had been able to unearth evidence of official misconduct, it would not have saved the Metropolitan, which was on a fast track toward destruction.[30]

As the year went on, letters continued to pour into the *Star* and *Tribune*, almost all of them calling for the Metropolitan to be spared from the wrecking ball. In September sixteen of the nation's leading architectural historians signed a letter urging the city of Minneapolis to acquire the building and "protect it for future generations." Among the signers was Philip Johnson, whose architectural firm a decade later would design Minneapolis's greatest twentieth-century

Demonstrators in historic costumes outside the Metropolitan Building, 1961. The Metropolitan's owner, Mel Hansen, organized the protests in a futile effort to save the building.

skyscraper—the IDS Building—which, like the Metropolitan, offered a large skylit court.[31]

The HRA, however, remained adamant, trotting out the same dubious arguments it had employed for years in defending its decision to raze the Metropolitan. Charles Horn, the HRA's chairman, suggested it would cost $2.2 million—a wildly inflated figure—to renovate the building up to modern standards. He went on to claim, despite a public statement to the contrary from IBM, that the corporation "very definitely" would not construct its planned building in the Gateway "if the Metropolitan Building stays." Horn also noted that the Sheraton-Ritz Hotel project was already behind schedule and asked, "Does Minneapolis want to delay and jeopardize the whole redevelopment plan?"[32]

Two days after Horn was quoted in the *Star*, the newspaper published a long memo from the HRA's attorney, Ben Palmer, listing six reasons, some of which were utterly bogus, as to why the Metropolitan could not possibly be allowed to stand. Aside from it being a visual "monstrosity," the building was guilty of many sins in Palmer's eyes. Among them: It was "70 years old," it was built with stone walls that made its structure "inflexible," and its layout was "inefficient." And, like Horn, Palmer could not resist the questionable contention that many of the wonderful new buildings being planned for the Gateway might never appear if they had to suffer the presence of the Metropolitan in all of its hoary decrepitude.[33]

With the HRA depicting the Metropolitan as an antiquated obstacle to progress, there was little real support in city government for any last-ditch effort to save the building. A few modest attempts were made, however. In September recently elected Minneapolis mayor Arthur Naftalin promised to "explore every possibility" for saving the Metropolitan. Nothing came of his efforts. In October Robert Bliss, an architect who taught at the University of Minnesota and who was also a member of the Save the Met committee, asked the HRA for permission to sandblast a small section of the building's sandstone walls to remove the soot and grime built up over many years. The thought apparently was that the walls would look so lovely the HRA would change its mind. It didn't. In November Robert McGregor, a city councilman, proposed a study to see if the building could be used by the city, but his motion failed on a nine-to-four vote.[34]

All of these last-minute efforts had a desperate air about them because the firing squad had already leveled its rifles and was not interested in pleas for mercy. The Metropolitan Building, guilty of old age if nothing else, was about to be executed, and it was all perfectly legal. So it was that on September 12, 1961, Hennepin District Court judge Luther Sletten approved a so-called quick take of the building by the HRA, under which the agency could assume immediate ownership even if the price to be paid for the Metropolitan remained in dispute. After refusing the HRA's last offer of $690,000, Hansen went back to court in June 1963—a year after the building had been demolished—and won a final settlement of $740,000, still far less than what he thought it was worth.[35]

~

Once the HRA took possession of the building in September 1961, it did not survive for long. Within little more than a month, all tenants—among them Wheeler and Hansen—were evicted. In his last letter to the HRA in July, Wheeler had written, "If you permit the Metropolitan Building to be destroyed, Minneapolis will

*"A Monstrosity in the Eyes of Most Observers"*

Two boys look down into the light court, 1961. Many people came for a last look at the Metropolitan after the Minneapolis Housing and Redevelopment Authority condemned the building.

lose a nationally famous and irreplaceable example of American architecture." But like all of Wheeler's pleas, it did no good, and in October he was forced out of the building where he had maintained his offices for forty-five years. Hansen, meanwhile, stayed on until he was the building's last occupant, alone on the twelfth floor, waiting for the day of destruction. When he finally left at the end of October, he did so with a flourish. Sitting in his desk chair, he was carried from the building like a deposed king, defiant to the end. "It is only people with weak minds who could think of wrecking it," he had once said of the Metropolitan. But in truth the forces arrayed against the building were anything but weak, and their day of triumph was about to come.[36]

In its last months, the doomed building became the scene of a prolonged wake, and visitors of all kinds stopped by for one last look at the remains. Some of the state's finest photographers—among them Jerome Liebling, Robert Jacobson, Robert Gene Wilcox, and Edwin Hirschoff—took stunning images of the

Workers demolish the roof of the Metropolitan Building, February 1962. The First National Bank Building, completed just two years earlier, rises in the distance, as does the Foshay Tower.

Demolition of the Metropolitan Building, from near Third Street and Nicollet Avenue, 1962. The building's picturesque rooftop, with its four corner towers, is already gone. Because of its proximity to the new U.S. Courthouse, the Metropolitan had to be razed very carefully, a process that took eight months.

building as the end neared. So, too, did a young filmmaker from the University of Minnesota named Edward Goldbarg. His ten-minute farewell included a haunting scene filmed in one of the building's elevators as it rose through the silent, empty light court.[37]

On December 7 the HRA awarded a $142,000 contract to Chies Brothers, a small company based in New Brighton, Minnesota, to wreck the building. Five days later, the city issued a demolition permit. On December 19, a day before the wrecking crews arrived, the *Tribune* offered an obituary of sorts. "Few persons will rejoice as the wrecking process begins," the newspaper wrote. "Many will experience a keen sense of anguish, a feeling of personal loss, as if a distinguished friend, heavy with the weight of years, had met an undeserved doom." Even so,

(*Above*) Cleared site of the Metropolitan Building, September 1962. This photograph appeared in the *Minneapolis Tribune* under a simple but affecting headline: "The Met Is No More." (*Left*) Ruins of the Metropolitan Building from Third Street and Second Avenue South, 1962. The ruins briefly stood as the last tangible reminder of a building that had once been one of the wonders of the city.

the writer argued that the building's destruction was necessary because it was being "sacrificed to one of the most badly needed urban redevelopment programs that ever promised to replace the blight and obsolescence of a skid-row area with order and beauty and economic stability."[38]

The "beauty" of the new Gateway would prove to be an illusion, and so too would the argument that the Metropolitan had to be "sacrificed" for the sake of progress. There was simply no good reason to destroy it, but that did not matter to the wreckers, who had a contract to fulfill. Over a span of eight months photographers documented the building's demise as floor by floor and stone by stone, Louis Menage's magnificent dream turned to dust. By August 1962 the Metropolitan—proud king of the Gateway—was gone, the last of its stone hauled away, and only a bare patch of ground remaining where once there had stood a thing of wonder.[39]

Men watch as the Metropolitan comes down, 1962. Virtually all of the Gateway's historic build-ings and haunts were gone by 1963. Its residents vanished as well, relocated to new homes around the city.

Among those who gathered to witness the Metropolitan's destruction were a few of the Gateway's old denizens, who by then were awaiting their own removal from the place they had long called home. Photographs show the men lounging across the street as cranes and wrecking balls chewed at the grand old pile. As they watched the building reduced at last to ruins, perhaps the old-timers felt, as did so many others in Minneapolis, a slight perturbation rippling through the soul of the city, as faint and inconsolable as the whisper of a passing ghost.

*"A Monstrosity in the Eyes of Most Observers"*

# EPILOGUE

# "The Most Unfortunate Thing"

The story of the Metropolitan Building did not end with its destruction. Much of its interior, including ironwork, light fixtures, and custom door hardware, was salvaged and then sold. Don Chies, whose firm wrecked the Metropolitan, said within a week of the time demolition began in December 1961 he had already heard from two hundred people seeking pieces of the building. The Metropolitan's superb trove of decorative ironwork, mostly in the form of railings and elevator grilles, was especially prized. Chies ultimately sold an estimated 1,500 lineal feet of ironwork to collectors, builders, and homeowners eager to possess a piece of history. Homeowners looking for accent pieces snapped up much of the ironwork. There were also some larger purchasers, among them the builder of a new motel in Hudson, Wisconsin, who bought 350 lineal feet of railings for use in a restaurant.[1]

Some of the huge, handsomely carved blocks of granite that formed the lower walls of the building were also salvaged. The owner of a stone yard in Delano, Minnesota, bought about 250 blocks in all, hoping to refabricate some of them for use in monuments or new building projects. But the blocks came in odd sizes, making them difficult to reuse. For the next fifty years, they rested in the stone yard like a pile of old dark bones. After new owners took over the stone business in 2010, some of the blocks were finally sold and then refashioned to become benches and walls in Ice House Plaza, which opened in 2012 on Nicollet Avenue near Twenty-Sixth Street in Minneapolis.[2]

Ironwork from the Metropolitan Building, 1962. Collectors eagerly snapped up railings, light fixtures, doorknobs, and other items salvaged from the building. Mrs. Marvin Montgomery, shown here, bought a row of railings to install on a balcony in her Edina home.

The building lives on as well in an exceptional body of photography. Nearly four hundred images of the building, ranging from distant views to close-up shots of ornamental details, can be found in local archives, and many more photographs doubtless exist in private collections. No other lost building in Minnesota has a visual record even remotely comparable in size.

The building has also come to occupy an important place in what might be called the civic imagination. It was featured on the cover of this author's 1992 book *Lost Twin Cities*, which was later turned into a popular public television

(*Above top*) Reused granite blocks from the Metropolitan Building at Ice House Plaza, designed in conjunction with Julie Snow Architects, Minneapolis, circa 2010. Massive granite blocks from the building's lower floors sat for years in a stone yard in Delano, Minnesota. (*Above*) Photographer at work on the top floor of the Metropolitan Building, 1961. Some of Minnesota's best photographers were drawn to the building as its demolition approached, and they left behind an extensive visual record of E. Townsend Mix's masterpiece.

documentary. Since then, the Metropolitan has continued to inspire writers, filmmakers, and artists, and it even has its own Facebook page maintained by a Minneapolis architect.[3]

~

Although the destruction of the Metropolitan was a wrenching blow to Minneapolis, its loss—and that of other monuments like New York City's magnificent Pennsylvania Station, razed in 1963—helped inspire new federal legislation aimed at preserving historic buildings and places. Just four years after the Metropolitan came down, Congress passed the National Historic Preservation Act, which not only created the National Register of Historic Places but also led to the establishment of historic districts in Minneapolis and most other American cities. As of 2018, Minneapolis had seventeen historic districts and more than 150 officially designated historic properties.[4]

Even so, notable buildings continue to fall, in Minneapolis and elsewhere. Ralph Rapson, who opposed the Metropolitan's destruction, lived long enough to see his most famous work—the Guthrie Theater—demolished in 2006 despite a robust campaign to save it, and other preservation battles are sure to come. When they do, the Metropolitan may well hover over the debate like a ghost in the room, serving not only as a potent symbol of loss but as a constant reminder of the importance of preservation.

Although the ghost cannot be restored to reality, it is not hard to imagine what would have happened had the Metropolitan escaped the Gateway Center project. It almost surely would have been designated a historically significant

The Metropolitan as it might look today in downtown Minneapolis. Had the building survived another ten years, it almost surely would have been renovated and restored.

building and may even have qualified as a National Historic Landmark. Nor is there much doubt it would have been refurbished and restored, especially after historic tax credits became available in the 1970s. Today, standing proud amid the dreary architecture of the remade Gateway, it would be regarded as one of the indelible marvels of the city.

~

But of course the Metropolitan didn't survive and by the time the last bits of the building were carted away in August 1962, much of the old Gateway was already gone as well. The HRA reported in December that it had already razed 176 buildings within the Gateway Center project area while relocating twenty-three hundred former residents to new housing elsewhere in the city. Building demolitions would continue into 1963, when the work of clearance was finally complete.[5]

Yet it took longer than expected to fill in all of the vacant blocks left behind by the renewal project. The site of the Metropolitan Building, by a certain bitter irony, was among the very last in the project area to be redeveloped. The HRA, having spent close to a million dollars to do away with the building, sold the cleared lot for $32,000, and it became, as Melvin Hansen ruefully put it, "one of the most expensive parking lots in the history of Minneapolis." It remained a parking lot until 1980, when the site was finally filled by a nondescript eight-story office building that seemed like a cruel insult to the memory of the Metropolitan.[6]

Hansen was still living when the Metropolitan's banal replacement finally appeared, but by then he was a ruined man. His long campaign against the HRA had cost him close to $100,000 in legal fees, and his fortune vanished with the building he loved. Forced to sell his palatial home in Golden Valley, where he'd once staged many memorable parties, Hansen by the 1980s was living alone in a small Minneapolis apartment. Until his dying day, which came in 1984 at age eighty-eight, he could not get over what had happened. The demolition of the Met, he said, was "a desecration and an abomination that will be deeply regretted in years to come." It is hard to disagree with that sentiment.[7]

Hansen's chief nemesis, Robert Jorvig of the HRA, also had some late thoughts about the Metropolitan and his agency's decision to destroy it. In a 1982 interview with a journalist named Sallie Stephenson, Jorvig admitted that the Metropolitan was "an attractive building" and claimed, "I was in favor of saving

330 Second Avenue South, 1980. The site of the Metropolitan remained a parking lot until 1980, when this run-of-the-mill office building finally filled the vacancy.

it myself." But he went on to argue, as he had more than twenty years earlier, that the HRA in effect had no choice when it came to demolishing the Metropolitan because, without numerous costly upgrades, the building could not have met modern standards required for all new construction in Gateway Center. "Ultimately, we had to have a solution that assured that the building was fixed up, compatible with the rest of the environment. Or we had to tear it down."[8]

Yet as had been the case years before, Jorvig struggled to explain why the Metropolitan had to be included in the Gateway Center project in the first place. By virtue of its size and architectural splendor, the Metropolitan was in every way a special case among the buildings of the historic Gateway. Moreover, Gateway Center's boundaries, which shifted several times before reaching their final form, had been drawn very precisely to exclude another large, historic office building—the Lumber Exchange. The Metropolitan, which, like the Lumber Exchange, was near the edge of the redevelopment area's boundaries, could just as easily have been left out.

Stephenson raised this issue in the interview. "If the Metropolitan hadn't been located in the Gateway area, if it had been located somewhere else in Minneapolis, then the building would have been left alone and it would probably still be functioning."

"It might have, yes," Jorvig acknowledged.

"Probably the most unfortunate thing was that it happened to be in your project area," Stephenson added.

A transcript of the interview reveals only a "pause" at this point, with no response from Jorvig, perhaps because there was nothing more to be said.

# Acknowledgments

More than a quarter of a century ago I wrote the book *Lost Twin Cities*, which attempted to resurrect some of the built history of Minneapolis and St. Paul. When the time came to select a cover photograph for that book, the choice seemed easy: it simply had to be the Metropolitan Building and its magnificent light court. Although the Metropolitan, better known as the Met, had been gone for thirty years by 1992, when *Lost Twin Cities* was published, the building still seemed alive in the public imagination. It was, in a very Minnesota sort of way, the architectural equivalent of the trophy fish that slipped the hook, never to be seen again but never to be forgotten either.

I was among those who could not forget the Met. I saw the building and its famous light court only once, in 1960 or 1961, when I was about fourteen years old. My father, who was born, raised, and died in Minneapolis, and who worked downtown his entire life, knew the building well and took me to see it, probably because he had heard it was about to come down. The experience is a fading memory now, a series of flickering impressions: the court opening into view, elevators climbing through their iron cages, glass floors aglow with light. My most vivid recollection is standing on the twelfth floor and looking down to the bottom of the court, where a few people scurried about. It all seemed wondrous then, and it still hurts to think that something so extraordinary was destroyed.

Decades later, as I learned more about the Met while working on *Lost Twin Cities*, I began to toy with the idea of writing a book about the building. Other projects intervened; a rather famous consulting detective from London occupied my attention for a number of years, and then there were books about all manner of things, from old crimes to lost mansions to the architectural world of the 1950s. But a pause finally came in 2016, and that's when the Met and its extraordinary story began tugging at me like an insistent child, demanding my attention.

I began my research for *Metropolitan Dreams* at the Minneapolis Central Library, home to the James K. Hosmer Special Collections. There, in the Minneapolis History Collection, I found a wealth of newspaper clippings, historic documents, and photographs relating to the Met. Ted Hathaway and other staff members were unfailingly helpful as I dug through the files and tried to learn all that I could about the building and its history.

Later, I pursued more information at other libraries around the Twin Cities. Among those I wish to thank for their assistance are Cheryll Fong, assistant curator at the Northwest Architectural Archives at the University of Minnesota; Susan Larson-Fleming, archivist at the Hennepin History Museum in Minneapolis; and the library staff at the Minnesota Historical Society in St. Paul.

I would like to thank other individuals as well. Ted Wright, a Minneapolis architect, generously made available his copy of a rarely seen book about the Met. He also maintains a wonderful website devoted to the building. Janet Olson shared memories about her uncle, Melvin Hansen, who once owned the Met and fought tenaciously to save it. Frederick Bentz and Milo Thompson, two distinguished Minneapolis architects, provided recollections of their days as young designers working for the firm of Thorshov and Cerny, which had offices in the Met.

I thank Erik Anderson and Kristian Tvedten at the University of Minnesota Press for their work in shepherding the book to publication. Kristian was especially helpful in the complicated process of gathering the book's illustrations.

Finally, as always, I own a special debt of gratitude to my wife, my partner, my lover, and my undisputed editor in chief, Jodie Ahern.

# Notes

## Introduction

1. *Minneapolis Star*, Dec. 20, 1961; *Minneapolis Tribune*, Dec. 17, 1961.
2. *Minneapolis Tribune*, Dec. 19, 1961, 1.

## 1. "Risen like an Exhalation"

1. *Minneapolis Tribune*, Jan. 1, 1889, 1.
2. Montgomery Schuyler, "Glimpses of Western Architecture: St. Paul and Minneapolis," *Harper's*, October 1891, reprinted in Montgomery Schuyler, *American Architecture and Other Writings*, ed. William H. Jordy and Ralph Coe (New York: Athenaeum, 1964), 126–27.
3. *Minneapolis Tribune*, Jan. 1, 1889, 1.
4. Robert M. Fogelson, *Downtown: Its Rise and Fall, 1880–1950* (New Haven, Conn.: Yale University Press, 2001), 12–13, 21.
5. Russell L. Olson, *The Electric Railways of Minnesota* (Hopkins: Minnesota Transportation Museum, 1976), 27.
6. *Minneapolis Tribune*, Jan. 1, 1887, 2.
7. *Minneapolis Tribune*, Jan. 1, 1889, 2.
8. Lucile M. Kane, *The Falls of St. Anthony: The Waterfall That Built Minneapolis* (St. Paul: Minnesota Historical Society Press, 1987), 107, 115.
9. *Minneapolis Tribune*, Jan. 1, 1881, 6.
10. *Minneapolis City Directory, 1893–94* (Detroit: R. L. Polk, 1894), 45.
11. Loring M. Staples, *The West Hotel Story* (Minneapolis: Carlson Printing, 1979), 87–92.
12. Larry Millett, *Lost Twin Cities* (St. Paul: Minnesota Historical Society Press, 1992), 156–58. The Syndicate Block was extensively remodeled after a fire in 1911 and again in 1959, when it was home to a J. C. Penney Department Store. It was torn down in 1989 to make way for a new retail development.
13. Ibid., 98–99.
14. *Saturday Evening Spectator*, Aug. 18, 1888, 6.
15. Penny A. Petersen, *Minneapolis Madams: The Lost History of Prostitution on the Riverfront* (Minneapolis: University of Minnesota Press, 2013), 77–79, 84.
16. *Minneapolis Tribune*, Oct. 4, 1888, 5.

## 2. "A Man of Peculiar Genius and Business Methods"

1. Isaac Atwater, ed., *History of the City of Minneapolis, Minnesota*, 2 vols. (New York: Munsell, 1893), 1:309–11; Loring Staples, "The Decline and Fall of Louis Menage," *Hennepin County History*, Spring 1983, 3–17; *Minneapolis Tribune*, Aug. 12, 1873, 1.
2. *Minneapolis Tribune*, Apr. 21, 1872, 4.
3. *Chicago Tribune*, June 23, 1895, 14.
4. Muriel Christison, "Leroy S. Buffington and the Minneapolis Building Boom of the 1880s," *Minnesota History* 23, no. 2 (1942): 219.
5. *Minneapolis Tribune*, Mar. 24, 1874, 5, and May 26, 1874, 1.
6. David A. Lanegran and Ernest R. Sandeen, *The Lake District of Minneapolis: A History of the Calhoun-Isles Community* (St. Paul: Living Historical Museum, 1979), 16, 37.
7. Atwater, *History of the City of Minneapolis*, 1:309–11.
8. Staples, "Decline and Fall of Louis Menage," 5–6; *Minneapolis Tribune*, May 19, 1929; *Minneapolis Star*, Feb. 27, 1956.
9. Larry Millett, *Once There Were Castles: Lost Mansions and Estates of the Twin Cities* (Minneapolis: University of Minnesota Press, 2011), 269–72.
10. Staples, "Decline and Fall of Louis Menage," 5–6.
11. *Daily Minnesota Tribune*, Sept. 4, 1883, 1, 6–8.
12. Staples, "Decline and Fall of Louis Menage," 6–10.
13. Atwater, *History of the City of Minneapolis*, 1:310.
14. *Minneapolis Times*, Feb. 23, 1895, 1.
15. Ellwood S. Hand, *The Northwestern Guaranty Loan Company's Building* (New York: Exhibit Publishing, 1890), n.p.
16. *Minneapolis Tribune*, Sept. 24, 1893, 6.
17. *St. Paul Daily Globe*, Sept. 22, 1893, 3.
18. Atwater, *History of the City of Minneapolis*, 1:311.
19. *Minneapolis Tribune*, Sept. 20, 1893, 1–2.
20. Richard Broderick, "Erased from Memory," *Rake*, May 20, 2005.
21. Staples, "Decline and Fall of Louis Menage," 12.
22. *Seattle Post-Intelligencer*, Aug. 24, 1893.
23. *Minneapolis Tribune*, Sept. 20, 1893, 1–2.

## 3. "One of the Great Architects of the Day"

1. Paul Clifford Larson, *Municipal Monument: A Centennial History of the Municipal Building Serving Minneapolis and Hennepin County, Minnesota* (Minneapolis: Municipal Building Commission, 1991), 19–25.
2. Kerck Kelsey, *Prairie Lightning: The Rise and Fall of William Drew Washburn* (Lakeville, Minn.: Pogo Press, 2010), 142.
3. David C. Smith, "Frederick Law Olmsted and Minneapolis Parks: Part 2," *Minneapolis Park History* (blog), June 14, 2013.

4. Millett, *Once There Were Castles*, 218–25.

5. *St. Paul Daily Globe*, Sept. 24, 1890, 8. Mix's only fully extant building in Minnesota is the Dodge County Courthouse in Mantorville, completed in 1871, well before he moved to Minneapolis. Portions of his Lowry Arcade (1893) in downtown St. Paul also survive, but the building has been so heavily remodeled that nothing of Mix's original design remains.

6. Frank Abial Flower, *History of Milwaukee, Wisconsin* (Chicago: Western Historical Company, 1881), 1499–1500.

7. Chris Szczesny-Adams, "The Mark of Mix," *Wisconsin People & Ideas*, Spring 2008, 33–34.

8. Howard Louis Conard, ed., *History of Milwaukee County from Its First Settlement to the Year 1895*, 2 vols. (Chicago: American Biographical Publishing, 1895), 2:445–48.

9. John Richard Burrows, "The Work of E. Townsend Mix from 1856–1890: A Study of His Artistic Development and His Relationship with the Yankee Society of the City of Milwaukee" (master's thesis, University of Virginia, 1980).

10. Sarah Bradford Landau and Carl W. Condit, *Rise of the New York Skyscraper, 1865–1913* (New Haven, Conn.: Yale University Press, 1996), 62–71.

11. Louis Sullivan, "The Tall Office Building Artistically Considered," in *Kindergarten Chats and Other Writings* (New York: Dover, 1979), 206. Sullivan's essay originally appeared in *Lippincott's Magazine*, Mar. 1896.

12. Carol Willis, *Form Follows Finance: Skyscrapers and Skylines in New York and Chicago* (New York: Princeton Architectural Press, 1995), 24–25.

13. Joseph J. Koran Jr., *The American Skyscraper, 1850–1940: A Celebration of Height* (Wellesley, Mass.: Brandon Books, 2008), 173–76.

14. The six-story Gilfillan Block, built in 1882 at 328 Jackson Street in St. Paul, was among the earliest office buildings with a skylit lobby in the Twin Cities. Later examples included the National Bank of Commerce (1889) and New York Life Building (1890) in Minneapolis, and the New York Life and Germania Life Buildings (both 1889) in St. Paul. All are long gone.

15. Millett, *Lost Twin Cities*, 86–87.

16. *Minneapolis Tribune*, Dec. 1, 1891, 2.

17. *St. Paul Daily Globe*, May 1, 1887, 1; Millett, *Lost Twin Cities*, 188–89.

18. For more on the Pioneer Building, see Larry Millett, *Heart of St. Paul: A History of the Pioneer and Endicott Buildings* (St. Paul: Minnesota Museum of American Art, 2016).

19. The Globe Building in Minneapolis never appears to have been very successful and had become a vacant hulk by the 1930s. Sold for back taxes in 1942, it was then converted into what must surely have been the most unusual parking garage in the city. It was still serving as a garage at the time it was demolished. See Millett, *Lost Twin Cities*, 200–201.

20. Atwater, *History of the City of Minneapolis*, 1:278.

21. *Minneapolis Tribune*, Nov. 28, 1888, 5. Charles Ferrin (1853–1929) had a long career in the Twin Cities. He did extensive work for Thomas Lowry, one of Louis Menage's

closest associates, serving as architect and superintendent for Lowry's Twin City Rapid Transit Company from 1900 to 1910. See Alan Lathrop, *Minnesota Architects: A Biographical Dictionary* (Minneapolis: University of Minnesota Press, 2010), 72–73.

22.  *Saturday Evening Spectator*, Feb. 2, 1889, 5.
23.  *Bulletin of the General Contractors Association*, October 1921, 17.
24.  *Minneapolis Journal*, May 31, 1890, 2.
25.  *Minneapolis Tribune*, Aug. 5, 1889, 5.
26.  *Minneapolis Tribune*, Nov. 22, 1889, 5.

## 4. "The Best Office Building in the World"

1.  *St. Paul and Minneapolis Pioneer Press*, June 1, 1890, 7.
2.  *Minneapolis Journal*, May 31, 1890, 1.
3.  *Minneapolis Tribune*, June 1, 1890, 1.
4.  *St. Paul and Minneapolis Pioneer Press*, June 1, 1890, 7.
5.  *Minneapolis Tribune*, June 1, 1890, 1.
6.  *St. Paul and Minneapolis Pioneer Press*, June 1, 1890, 7; *Minneapolis Tribune*, June 1, 1890, 1.
7.  *St. Paul Daily Globe*, Sept. 24, 1890, 8; *Minneapolis Tribune*, Sept. 24, 1890, 5. The three-story Arcade Building, also known as the Grand Arcade or the Lowry Arcade, was completed in 1893 and extended for an entire block between Fourth and Fifth Streets just west of Wabasha Street. It included a shopping arcade, the Field-Schlick Department Store and a large Masonic hall on the top floor. Portions of the building still stand along Fifth Street but Mix's original facade is long gone.
8.  *Minneapolis Journal*, May 31, 1890, 2.
9.  Among the large skyscrapers of note in other cities was the thirteen-story Chamber of Commerce Building in Chicago, which was completed in 1889 and included a light court taller than the Guaranty Loan's, although not as large or ornate. For more on the building, see Carl W. Condit, *American Building Art: The Nineteenth Century* (New York: Oxford University Press, 1960), 58–59.
10.  Millett, *Lost Twin Cities*, 214–15.
11.  Hand, *The Northwestern Guaranty Loan Company's Building*.
12.  Schuyler, "Glimpses of Western Architecture," 151.
13.  Patricia Anne Murphy, "The Early Career of Cass Gilbert: 1878 to 1895" (master's thesis, University of Virginia, 1979), 31.
14.  Steve Swenson and Rick Russack, "Redstone Granite Quarries," http://www.white mountainhistory.org/Redstone_Granite.html.
15.  Kathryn Bishop Eckert, *The Sandstone Architecture of the Lake Superior Region* (Detroit: Wayne State University Press, 2000), 70–79.
16.  Hand, *The Northwestern Guaranty Loan Company's Building*.
17.  *Minneapolis and the Guaranty Loan Building* (1892), 22.
18.  Jack El-Hai, *Lost Minnesota: Stories of Vanished Places* (Minneapolis: University of Minnesota Press, 2000), 32–35.

19. Hand, *The Northwestern Guaranty Loan Company's Building.*
20. Ibid., n.p.
21. *Minneapolis Tribune*, June 6, 1892, 1.
22. *Minneapolis Tribune*, Aug. 17, 1890, 10.
23. Millett, *Lost Twin Cities*, 224.
24. *Minneapolis Journal*, May 15, 1894, 1.

## 5. "One of the Most Colossal Swindles of the Decade"

1. *Minneapolis Tribune*, Oct. 1, 1893, 6.
2. *Minneapolis Tribune*, June 1, 1894, 8; June 6, 1894, 8; June 7, 1894, 8. The *Tribune* reported on Apr. 8, 1890, that Menage had in fact taken Burke to court, presumably for libel, but the outcome of the case isn't known.
3. *Minneapolis Tribune*, Oct. 2, 1893, 8; *St. Paul Daily Globe*, Dec. 2, 1893, 8. Burke harshly criticized Kenyon's report, claiming it was little better than a whitewash of the Guaranty Loan Company. According to a *Tribune* story on May 23, 1893, Kenyon responded by confronting Burke on the steps of the capitol in St. Paul and punching him in the nose.
4. *Minneapolis Journal*, Oct. 8, 1891, 5.
5. Douglas Steeples and David O. Whitten, *Democracy in Desperation: The Depression of 1893* (Westport, Conn.: Greenwood Press, 1998), 2–37, 42–53.
6. *Minneapolis Tribune*, Jan. 10, 1894, 5; E. Dudley Parsons, *The Story of Minneapolis* (Minneapolis: Author, 1913), 129.
7. *Minneapolis Tribune*, Sept. 20, 1893, 2.
8. *Minneapolis Journal*, Apr. 15, 1893, 1.
9. *Minneapolis Journal*, May 16, 1893; *New York Times*, May 28, 1893, 8.
10. *Minneapolis Tribune*, July 9, 1893, 2; *St. Paul Daily Globe*, July 13, 1893, 3.
11. *Minneapolis Tribune*, Aug. 13, 1893, 1; Oct. 1, 1893, 6.
12. Neither Guatemala nor Mexico had formal extradition treaties with the United States in 1893, which meant it would have been very difficult, especially given Menage's legal and financial resources, to bring him back to Minnesota for prosecution.
13. *Minneapolis Tribune*, May 29, 1893, 7; Sept. 20, 1893, 3; Oct. 1, 1893, 6.
14. *Seattle Post-Intelligencer*, Aug. 24, 1893.
15. *Minneapolis Tribune*, Sept. 20, 1893, 1–2; Sept. 21, 1891, 5.
16. *Minneapolis Tribune*, Sept. 20, 1893, 1–2.
17. *Minneapolis Tribune*, Sept. 29, 1893, 4.
18. *St. Paul Daily Globe*, Sept. 20, 1893, 3; *Minneapolis Tribune*, Sept. 23, 1893, 1.
19. *Minneapolis Tribune*, Sept. 29, 1893, 4.
20. *Minneapolis Tribune*, Dec. 2, 1893, 5.
21. *Minneapolis Tribune*, May 29, 1894, 3.
22. *Minneapolis Tribune*, June 1, 1894, 4; July 1, 1894, 5.
23. *Minneapolis Tribune*, July 1, 1894, 5.

24. *Minneapolis Tribune*, Nov. 25, 1894, 12; Dec. 5, 1894, 5.

25. For a thorough account of the Ging–Hayward case, see Shawn Francis Peters, *The Infamous Harry Hayward: A True Account of Murder and Mesmerism in Gilded Age Minneapolis* (Minneapolis: University of Minnesota Press, 2018).

26. *Minneapolis Times*, Feb. 23, 1895, 1–2.

27. Ibid., 2.

28. *Minneapolis Tribune*, Sept. 20, 1893, 1–2.

29. *St. Paul Daily Globe*, May 27, 1894, 10.

30. *Chicago Tribune*, June 23, 1895, 14.

31. *Minneapolis Tribune*, June 29, 1899, 5.

32. *Minneapolis Tribune*, Dec. 12, 1899, 5.

33. *Minneapolis Tribune*, Jan. 1, 1905, 5.

## 6. "The Lower Loop Is Sunk"

1. Joseph Hart, *Down & Out: The Life and Death of Minneapolis's Skid Row* (Minneapolis: University of Minnesota Press, 2002), 8–12.

2. David L. Rosheim, *The Other Minneapolis: A History of the Minneapolis Skid Row* (Maquoketa, Iowa: Andromeda Press, 1978), 42.

3. *Minneapolis Journal*, Dec. 2, 1906, editorial section, 1; Lathrop, *Minnesota Architects*, 111–12.

4. *Western Architect*, Dec. 1908, 64; Judith Martin, "Before and After the Bulldozers," in Robert B. Silberman and Judith Martin, *The Gateway* (Minneapolis: Minnesota Center for Book Arts, 1993), 4.

5. David C. Smith, *City of Parks: The Story of Minneapolis Parks* (Minneapolis: Foundation for Minneapolis Parks, 2008), 90–92.

6. *Minneapolis Tribune*, June 30, 1908, 7.

7. Vincent Oredson, "Planning a City: Minneapolis, 1907–17," *Minnesota History*, Winter 1953, 331–39.

8. Andrew Wright Crawford and Edward H. Bennett, *Plan of Minneapolis* (Minneapolis: Civic Commission, 1917).

9. Millett, *Lost Twin Cities*, 102, 292–93.

10. *Minneapolis Journal*, July 3, 1921, 2nd sec., 1; Millett, *Once There Were Castles*, 168–71, 176–80.

11. The four-thousand-seat Minnesota (Radio City) Theater was demolished in 1959. The Northwestern National Bank Building, heavily damaged by fire in 1982, was razed two years later. See Millett, *Lost Twin Cities*, 199, 298–99.

12. Rosheim, *Other Minneapolis*, 106–7. The Ritz (Minnesotan) Hotel was one of the earliest works of the Minneapolis architectural firm of Liebenberg and Kaplan, which later became best known for designing movie theaters throughout Minnesota. The hotel was demolished in 1963 as part of the Gateway Center urban renewal project.

13. The Pick-Nicollet Hotel closed in 1973. After being used as housing for several years, the building became vacant and was torn down in 1991.

14. Rosheim, *Other Minneapolis*, 21.

15. According to Davison's *Minneapolis City Directory* for 1922, twenty-four freight agents representing railroads from all across the country had offices in the Metropolitan Building. There were also nineteen real estate companies and about a half dozen law firms.

16. *St. Paul Daily Globe*, Oct. 8, 1900, 4.

17. *Minneapolis Journal*, Nov. 12, 1902, 6.

18. *Minneapolis Journal*, Mar. 17, 1924; *Minneapolis Tribune*, Mar. 18, 1924, 10; Staples, "Decline and Fall of Louis Menage," 15.

19. *Minneapolis Tribune*, Mar. 30, 1924.

20. *Minneapolis Journal*, Oct. 3, 1929.

21. Rosheim, *Other Minneapolis*, 120–21; Hart, *Down & Out*, 19–21.

22. Millett, *Once There Were Castles*, 193–96, 241–45.

23. Iric Nathanson, "The 1940 Marlborough Hotel Fire: 'There Was Nothing That Escaped the Flames,' " *MinnPost*, Jan. 3, 2013.

24. Judith A. Martin and Antony Goddard, *Past Choices/Present Landscapes: The Impact of Urban Renewal on the Twin Cities* (Minneapolis: Center for Urban and Regional Affairs, 1989), 33.

25. Petersen, *Minneapolis Madams*, 145–56; Rosheim, *Other Minneapolis*, 103, 117.

26. Smith, *City of Parks*, 147–49.

27. *Minneapolis Star Journal*, Aug. 25, 1940.

28. *Minneapolis Star Journal*, Feb. 25, 1940.

## 7. "How Sick Is This Heart of Minneapolis?"

1. Rebecca Lou Smith, *Postwar Housing in National and Local Perspective: A Twin Cities Case Study* (Minneapolis: Center for Urban and Regional Affairs, 1978), 1.

2. Iric Nathanson, "Housing and Redevelopment Authority: Clearing Urban Blight," *Hennepin History*, Winter 1988, 5–23.

3. Hart, *Down & Out*, 40–41; Lathrop, *Minnesota Architects*, 35.

4. Cerny's plan was published in pamphlet form as *Recommendations for the Development of the Lower Loop* (Minneapolis: Civic Center Development Association, 1945). See also *Minneapolis Tribune*, May 20, 1945, 1. As it turned out, the new federal courthouse was not the cause of the Metropolitan Building's destruction, as Cerny had imagined. Instead, the courthouse occupied only a half-block site and was finished just before the Metropolitan came down as part of the Gateway project.

5. Martin, "Before and After the Bulldozers," 5.

6. Sherman Hasbrouck, "A History of the Minneapolis Lower Loop" (unpublished manuscript, 1956), 10.

7. *Minneapolis Star*, Feb. 3, 1947.

8. *Minneapolis Star*, Aug. 9, 1946.

9. *Minneapolis Times*, Aug. 9, 1946.

10. *Minneapolis Star*, Mar. 12, 1966, 5A; author interview with Janet Olson (Melvin Hansen's niece), May 2, 2017; Kris Kemp (Hansen's granddaughter), unpublished manuscript, date unknown, copy in Minneapolis History Collection at Hennepin County Library.

11. Herman Olson, *A Plan for the Redevelopment of the Lower Loop Area* (Minneapolis: City Planning Commission, 1952).

12. Nathanson, "Housing and Redevelopment Authority," 8.

13. Martin and Goddard, *Past Choices/Present Landscapes*, 34–41.

14. *Minneapolis Star*, Sept. 30, 1953.

15. *Minneapolis Star*, Oct. 23, 1953.

16. *Minneapolis Star*, Feb. 26, 1954.

17. "Lower Loop" (unpublished document, Minneapolis Housing and Redevelopment Authority, Aug. 18, 1955).

18. John C. Teaford, *The Rough Road to Renaissance: Urban Revitalization in America, 1940–1985* (Baltimore: The Johns Hopkins University Press, 1990), 10–12.

19. *Minneapolis Star*, Dec. 9, 1959, 3D.

20. Daniel M. Abramson, *Obsolescence: An Architectural History* (Chicago: University of Chicago Press, 2016), 21–30, 42–43.

21. Ibid., 27–28.

22. Hart, *Down & Out*, 44; *Minneapolis Tribune*, Mar. 2, 1956, 10.

23. Larry Millett, *Minnesota Modern: Architecture and Life at Midcentury* (Minneapolis: University of Minnesota Press, 2015), 76–77.

24. Ibid., 82-87.

25. *Minneapolis Star*, July 25, 1955, 12.

26. *Minneapolis Tribune*, Jan. 8, 1956.

27. *Minneapolis Star*, Apr. 8, 1958, 1A.

28. *Minneapolis Star*, July 9, 1957.

29. *Minneapolis Tribune*, May 29, 1958.

30. *Gateway Center Urban Renewal Plan* (Minneapolis: Housing and Redevelopment Authority, 1958).

31. *Minneapolis Tribune*, Jan. 22, 1959.

32. Martin, "Before and After the Bulldozers," 5.

## 8. "A Monstrosity in the Eyes of Most Observers"

1. *Minneapolis Star*, Oct. 30, 1958.

2. Millett, *Lost Twin Cities*, 214–15.

3. *Minneapolis Star*, Sept. 13, 1961.

4. *Minneapolis Tribune*, Feb. 14, 1959; *Minneapolis Star*, Apr. 9, 1959.

5. *Minneapolis Star*, Apr. 9, 1959.

6. *Minneapolis Tribune*, Dec. 1, 1958.

7. *Minneapolis Star*, June 16, 1959.

8. *Minneapolis Tribune*, Dec. 14, 1958.

9. Lathrop, *Minnesota Architects*, 225; Walter Wheeler to the Minneapolis Housing and Redevelopment Authority, July 24, 1961, in Walter Hall Wheeler Papers, Northwest Architectural Archives, University of Minnesota Libraries, Minneapolis (hereafter Wheeler Papers).

10. Walter Wheeler to P. K. Peterson, July 25, 1949, Wheeler Papers.

11. A. C. Godward, "Preliminary Analysis and Report re. the Proposed Demolition of the Metropolitan Building," Aug. 11, 1959, Minneapolis History Collection, Hennepin County Library.

12. *Minneapolis Tribune*, Sept. 18, 1959.

13. *Minneapolis Star*, Dec. 10, 1959.

14. *Minneapolis Tribune*, June 27, 1959.

15. *Minneapolis Tribune*, Oct. 3, 1959.

16. The best record of the various court cases surrounding the Metropolitan Building in 1959 and 1960 can be found in *Housing and Redevelopment Authority for the City of Minneapolis vs. Minneapolis Metropolitan Corporation*, Minnesota Supreme Court, case file 38028, at the Minnesota Historical Society.

17. Walter Wheeler to State Rep. F. Gordon Wright, Feb. 9, 1960, Wheeler Papers.

18. Minnesota Supreme Court, case file 38028.

19. Hart, *Down & Out*, 45.

20. Senator Eugene McCarthy to Walter Wheeler, Dec. 1, 1961, Wheeler Papers; *Minneapolis Tribune*, Dec. 13, 1961.

21. *Minneapolis Star*, Sept. 9, 1961.

22. *Minneapolis Star*, Dec. 21, 1959; *Minneapolis Tribune*, Dec. 22, 1959; Minnesota Supreme Court, case file 38028.

23. *Minneapolis Star*, Aug. 5, 1960; Minnesota Supreme Court, case file 38028.

24. Patricia Cavanaugh, *Politics and Freeways: Building the Twin Cities Interstate System* (Minneapolis: Center for Urban and Regional Affairs, 2006); *Minneapolis Tribune*, Apr. 8, 1959.

25. *Gateway Center Progress Report*, 1961, Minneapolis Housing and Redevelopment Authority.

26. Hart, *Down & Out*, 49; *Minneapolis Star*, Apr. 23, 1959.

27. Rosheim, *Other Minneapolis*, 194.

28. Minneapolis Housing and Redevelopment Authority Board of Commissioners, meeting minutes, Apr. 1960.

29. *Minneapolis Star*, Oct. 23, 1959.

30. Senator Hubert H. Humphrey to Walter Wheeler, Jan. 16, 1961; Walter Wheeler to Frank Dunleavy, June 10, 1961; both, Wheeler Papers.

31. *Minneapolis Star*, Sept. 19, 1961.

32. *Minneapolis Star*, Sept. 7, 1961; *Minneapolis Tribune*, Dec. 13, 1961.

33. *Minneapolis Star*, Sept. 9, 1961.

34. *Minneapolis Tribune*, Sept. 1, 1961, Nov. 11, 1961; Minneapolis Housing and Redevelopment Authority Board of Commissioners, meeting minutes, Oct. 5, 1961.

35. *Minneapolis Tribune*, Sept. 13, 1961.

36. Walter Wheeler to Minneapolis Housing and Redevelopment Authority, July 24, 1961, Wheeler Papers; *Minneapolis Star*, Aug. 11, 1961, 11A.

37. The Minneapolis Institute of Art mounted a special exhibition of Jacobson's photographs of the Metropolitan Building in September 1961, just as the building was on the brink of demolition. Goldbarg's black-and-white film was not the only record of the building's last days. In August 1961 a traveling young architect who worked for the famed midcentury modernist Eero Saarinen took twenty-nine minutes of color film in and around the Metropolitan, including scenes of wrecking crews at work on the old U.S. Post Office next door. Both films can be found on YouTube.

38. *Minneapolis Tribune*, Dec. 8, 1961; Dec. 19, 1961.

39. *Minneapolis Tribune*, Sept. 23, 1962.

## Epilogue

1. *Minneapolis Star*, Dec. 28, 1961; *Minneapolis Tribune*, Nov. 18, 1962.

2. *Delano Herald-Journal*, May 21, 2010; *Minneapolis Tribune*, Nov. 2, 2011; *Twin Cities Daily Planet*, May 25, 2012.

3. Architect Theodore D. Wright created the Facebook page "Metropolitan Building Minneapolis" in 2013. It includes historic photographs, a partial floor plan, and much other information.

4. Like Minneapolis, New York City had no historic preservation commission or other agency in 1963 that might have been able to contest the demolition of Pennsylvania Station. See Lorraine B. Diehl, *The Late, Great Pennsylvania Station* (New York: American Heritage Press, 1985), 145.

5. Minneapolis Housing and Redevelopment Authority, annual report, Dec. 31, 1962.

6. *Minneapolis Tribune*, Sept. 6, 1980; *Minneapolis Star Tribune*, Dec. 10, 2011.

7. *Minneapolis Daily Herald*, July 25, 1962; *Minneapolis Star Tribune*, Aug. 27, 2017, H5.

8. Sallie Stephenson, "The Man Who Tore Down the Met," taped interview with Robert Jorvig, 1982, transcript in Minneapolis History Collection, Hennepin County Library.

# Illustration Credits

Photographs and illustrations in this book appear courtesy of the institutions and individuals listed here. Specific collections and the photographer's name, if known, are included in parentheses.

## Dana Wheelock Architectural Photography

Page 74 (copyright Dana Wheelock)

## DJR Architecture, Inc.

Page 219 (*top*)

## Jim Foster

Page 220–21

## Hennepin County Library

Pages 10–11 (Benjamin Franklin Upton); 13, 30, 32, 35, 43, 59 (John H. Kammerdiener); 92, 114 (*top*), 116 (*bottom*), 117 (*top*), 117 (*bottom*), 156, 160–61 (Robert C. Busch); 167, 174 (copyright *Star Tribune*); 182–83 (Don Berg); 186 (photograph by Dwight Miller, copyright *Star Tribune*); 188, 200, 205 (Floyd J. Kelly); 209, 211 (Robert Jacobson); 213 (Earl Chambers); 214–15 (Robert Jacobson); 223 (James Taulman)

## Hennepin History Museum

Page 216 (Edward Hirschoff)

## Library of Congress, Prints and Photographs Division

Pages vii (Detroit Publishing Company Collection); 45 *(above left)* (Brady-Handy Photograph Collection); 62–63 (Jack Boucher, Historic American Buildings Survey Collection); 66 *(above left)*, 76–77 (Detroit Publishing Company Collection); 90 (Jack Boucher, Historic American Buildings Survey Collection); 152 (George Grantham Bain Collection); 198 (Detroit Publishing Company Collection)

## Minneapolis Institute of Art

Page 2 (photograph by Robert Gene Wilcox, American, 1925–1970; gelatin silver print; Minneapolis Institute of Art, The Miscellaneous Works of Art Purchase Fund 74.72.16. Copyright Estate of Robert Gene Wilcox.)

## Minnesota Historical Society

Pages 4, 5 (Bill Seaman, *Minneapolis Star*); 6–7 (Robert Jacobson); 14–15 (William Henry Illingworth); 16, 18 (William H. Jacoby); 20, 22–23, 25, 27, 28 *(top)*, 28–29 (Sweet Studio); 31 (William H. Jacoby); 33 (*Minneapolis Star Journal*); 36 (Arthur B. Rugg); 38 (William W. Wales); 41 (Benjamin Franklin Upton); 45 *(above right)*, 46–47, 47 *(bottom)*, 48 (William H. Jacoby); 49, 51 (*Minneapolis Journal*); 54 *(above right)*, 56 (William H. Jacoby); 58, 65, 67 (Charles P. Gibson); 68–69 (William H. Jacoby); 70 (Norton & Peel); 71, 73 (T. W. Ingersoll); 75, 80, 82, 86 (C. J. Hibbard); 87 (Norton & Peel); 94–95 *(right)*, 97 (Henry Benbrooke Hall); 98–99 (Norton & Peel); 102, 103, 105, 106 (Robert Jacobson); 107 *(left)* (Norton & Peel); 107 *(right)* (Robert Jacobson); 110–11, 122, 123, 124, 128, 129, 132, 134–35, 136 (Norton & Peel); 138, 140, 141, 144–45, 147, 148–49 (C. J. Hibbard); 150 (*Minneapolis Star Journal*); 154–55 (*Minneapolis Star Journal*); 157, 158–59 (Joseph Zalusky); 166 (Norton & Peel); 168–69 (*Minneapolis Star Journal*); 171, 172 (Norton & Peel); 173 (*Minneapolis Star Journal*); 177 (*Minneapolis Star Journal*); 181, 190 (Henry Benbrooke Hall); 195 (Lee Brothers); 197 (C. J. Hibbard); 202 *(left)* (Robert Travis Keagle); 202–3, 206–7 (Norton & Peel); 212 (Gerald Brimacombe, *Minneapolis Tribune*); 218 (Wayne Bell, *Minneapolis Tribune*); 219 *(bottom)* (Robert Jacobson)

## New York Public Library

Pages 54 (*above left*) (Isaac Atwater, *History of the City of Minneapolis*, vol. 1, 309); 60 (*The National Cyclopaedia of American Biography*, 1898)

## Reyerson & Burnham Libraries, The Art Institute of Chicago

Pages 66 (*above right*) (*Inland Architect* 20, Reyerson & Burnham Archives, digital file #IA20XX_1109), 72 (Reyerson & Burnham Library & Archives, digital file #000000_19731_21_105), 94 (*left*) (Chicago Architectural Sketch Club Collection, Reyerson & Burnham Archives, digital file # casc.1892_73).

## Star Tribune News Archives

Pages 175, 185 (copyright Northwest Architectural Archives, University of Minnesota Libraries); 215 (*right*) (photo by Powell Kruger, copyright 1962 *Star Tribune*)

## University of Minnesota Libraries

Pages 24, 84, 89, 101 (Northwest Architectural Archives, University of Minnesota Libraries); 108 (*left*), 108 (*right*), 112, 114 (*bottom*), 115, 116 (*top*), 125, 146

# Index

Page numbers in **bold** refer to illustrations

**Larry Millett**, a native of Minneapolis, has spent much of his career as a writer, reporter, and editor for the *St. Paul Pioneer Press*. He became the newspaper's first architecture critic in 1985. His many books include *Lost Twin Cities, Once There Were Castles: Lost Mansions and Estates of the Twin Cities* (Minnesota, 2011), *Minnesota Modern: Architecture and Life at Midcentury* (Minnesota, 2015), *Minnesota's Own: Preserving Our Grand Homes*, and *Heart of St. Paul: A History of the Pioneer and Endicott Buildings*.